Family and Kinship in England 1450–1800

Family and Kinship in England 1450–1800

Will Coster

An imprint of **Pearson Education**

Harlow, England · London · New York · Reading, Massachusetts · San Francisco · Toronto · Don Mills, Ontario · Sydney
Tokyo · Singapore · Hong Kong · Seoul · Taipei · Cape Town · Madrid · Mexico City · Amsterdam · Munich · Paris · Milan

PEARSON EDUCATION LIMITED

Head Office:
Edinburgh Gate
Harlow CM20 2JE
Tel: +44 (0)1279 623623
Fax: +44 (0)1279 431059

London Office:
128 Long Acre
London WC2E 9AN
Tel: +44 (0)20 7447 2000
Fax: +44 (0)20 7240 5771
Website: www.history-minds.com

First published in Great Britain in 2001

© Pearson Education, 2001

ISBN 0 582 35717 9

British Library Cataloguing in Publication Data
A CIP catalogue record for this book can be obtained from the British Library

10 9 8 7 6 5 4 3 2 1

Set in 10/12 Sabon Roman by Graphicraft Limited, Hong Kong
Printed in Malaysia , LSP

The Publishers' policy is to use paper manufactured from sustainable forests.

CONTENTS

INTRODUCTION TO THE SERIES

Such is the pace of historical enquiry in the modern world that there is an ever-widening gap between the specialist article or monograph, incorporating the results of current research, and general surveys, which inevitably become out of date. *Seminar Studies in History* is designed to bridge this gap. The series was founded by Patrick Richardson in 1966 and his aim was to cover major themes in British, European and World history. Between 1980 and 1996 Roger Lockyer continued his work, before handing the editorship over to Clive Emsley and Gordon Martel. Clive Emsley is Professor of History at the Open University, while Gordon Martel is Professor of International History at the University of Northern British Columbia, Canada and Senior Research Fellow at De Montfort University.

All the books are written by experts in their field who are not only familiar with the latest research but have often contributed to it. They are frequently revised, in order to take account of new information and interpretations. They provide a selection of documents to illustrate major themes and provoke discussion, and also a guide to further reading. The aim of *Seminar Studies in History* is to clarify complex issues without over-simplifying them, and to stimulate readers into deepening their knowledge and understanding of major themes and topics.

NOTE ON REFERENCING SYSTEM

Readers should note that numbers in square brackets [5] refer them to the corresponding entry in the Bibliography at the end of the book (specific page numbers are given in italics). A number in square brackets preceded by *Doc.* [*Doc.* 5] refers readers to the corresponding item in the Documents section which follows the main text.

AUTHOR'S ACKNOWLEDGEMENTS

I am particularly grateful to Bill Sheils and Peter Marshall for their help and encouragement in undertaking this work. Further thanks are due to Professor Claire Cross and Dr Ralph Houlbrooke for their direction and support. I would also like to thank my students over the last decade, in my time as a W. E. A. tutor at York, and also those who took my third-year course on the family at Bedford, between 1994 and 2000, whose enthusiasm and criticism has done much to form my own ideas about the history of the family and its study. My greatest debt remains to my wife Caroline, who read, commented on and corrected the text. Finally, I would like to thank my parents, to whom this book is dedicated.

PUBLISHER'S ACKNOWLEDGEMENTS

We are grateful to the following for permission to reproduce copyright material:

The Board of Trustees of the Victoria & Albert Museum for the two Memorial Brasses reproduced in the Document Section, p. 132.

The Mary Evans Picture Library for supplying the following images for the plate section:

1. 'The position of the foetus in the womb immediately prior to delivery', Ebinezer Sibly Dodd, A Key to Physic and the Occult Sciences, 1794. 10029818/02
2. 'The Happy Marriage', engraving by T. Ryder after William Hogarth. 10036986/02
3. 'Wife goes for her husband with a kitchen utensil, he protects his head as best he can', woodcut illustration to the Roxburghe Ballads, vol. 2, part 1, p. 5 versa, c. 1630. 10067654/02
4. 'A Puritan family . . .' Woodcut engraving from 'The Whole Psalms in Four Parts', 1563. 10046505/05
5. 'Father reads by candlelight to his wife and their six children in a well-to-do household', Dodd, engraving by T. Cook, 1763. 10057660/05
6. 'A skeleton and a skull and crossbones', woodcut illustration to the Roxburghe Ballads, vol. 1, part 2, p. 398, c. 1640. 10067643/03
7. 'Funeral of a well-to-do English individual . . .' Bernard Picat, Religious Ceremonies of the World, 1731. 10052475/04
8. 'Country people leaving a village due to enclosures', unattributed engraving, 18th Century. 10037482/03

PART ONE

INTRODUCTION – METHODS AND STRUCTURES

CHAPTER ONE

APPROACHING THE HISTORY OF THE FAMILY

Thirty years ago, family life in the past was largely of interest only to some literary historians, antiquarians and those concerned with their own genealogies. Today the family is among the essential areas of academic historical interest. This is nowhere more true than for England in the early modern period, between the close of the middle ages and the beginnings of industrialisation, an era which has often been seen as a watershed in patterns of social organisation.

The rapidly expanding investigation of the social history of early modern England over the last fifty years, has indicated most clearly that it was a highly complex and diverse society. In theory, the way society was organised was simple and unchanging, but in reality, there was a mixture of continuity and change and considerable local diversity and complexity. In the recent past, many historians adopted a Marxist framework (even when they did not accept Marxist politics or terminology) to explain this change. This depicted the period as one of transition from a feudal, land-based society, divided between a rural aristocracy and a peasantry, to one founded on capital and industry, where the great social divisions were between an emerging middle class and an increasingly industrialised working class or proletariat. This process was seen as having particular significance, since the engine of this change, the Industrial Revolution that began in the eighteenth century, was the first of its kind, and therefore the model for future European and world history. In understanding the history of the family in this period it is important to appreciate how dominant these ideas have been. It is also necessary to digest, at least to a degree, how this grand picture has fragmented in recent years, a process in which the study of the family has played a very significant part.

Today, most historians are reluctant to use the terms feudal, class or industrialisation without extreme care. The society of late medieval England was certainly based to a large degree on land ownership, but it was far from classically feudal. The dramatic return to England of the bubonic plague in the Black Death of 1348–49, and its frequent re-visitations thereafter, was one major factor. The plague helped reduce the population and created much short-term suffering, but it also led to shortages of labour that benefited the descendants of the majority of survivors. The results were greater freedom, higher standards of living for many and, arguably, greater economic opportunities.

Partly as a result of these factors, by the beginning of our period society already looked far more complex than the simple image of the lord in his manor house and his immobile peasants tied to the land. At the top of the social order there was still a landed aristocracy, but it ranged widely in wealth and status. There were the great families, many holding hereditary titles and enormous estates, but there were also many smaller landholders, often styling themselves as gentlemen, who did not enjoy hereditary titles but tended to dominate a group of communities, or a single rural community. Below them most villages had a handful of significant landholders, usually described as yeomen, who ran agricultural holdings large enough to need the employment of the labour of others. Beneath them were the small landholders, often termed husbandmen, who might employ others, but usually carried out a large portion of the labour needed on their own land, and often pursued another occupation, such as blacksmith or tanner. These two groups of smaller landholders are often placed together (along with their counterparts in the towns: the merchants, traders and independent craftsmen) as the 'middling sort'. What made them the middle of the social order was the existence below them of the majority of the population, which may be best described as the poor. These ranged from relatively stable labourers, who might own small plots of land, but were largely dependent on working for others, to a large group of landless, and often workless, vagrants. This last group horrified Tudor and Stuart commentators by roaming the highways and trails of the country in search of employment and food. This, then, was not a society of a few clearly defined classes, but of many inter-locking social orders.

That is not to say that it was a static society, far from it. It was possible for members of one social order to move up, with success, into higher social groups, and it was just as possible for them or their descendants to move down. In understanding the care and concern that marked early modern attitudes to status and property in the family, it is worth bearing in mind that the fear of just such a fate haunted virtually all those who had anything at all. As we shall see, one clear pattern across our period is the virtual disappearance of small landholders from local records and the growth of those groups that made up the landless poor. Part of the reason for this was the return to population expansion that was beginning at the opening of our period. In the mid-fifteenth century, England and Wales had approximately two million inhabitants. By the middle of the sixteenth, it was around three million and by the middle of the seventeenth, it had passed five, thereby reaching what was probably the level it had enjoyed before the Black Death. Thereafter numbers fluctuated and even fell, but there was a return to expansion by the end of our period. By the late eighteenth century, the take-off associated with industrialisation had begun and there were already over eight and a half million inhabitants in England and Wales.

If the fall in population in the late medieval period raised standards of living, then inevitably such a dramatic rise was likely to decrease them. The result still looks something like the Marxist observation of the creation of a small elite who controlled economic production and the majority who worked for them. Such massive changes, it seems, must have produced a fundamental transformation in the nature of the family, and how this transformation fitted into this wider picture became one of the great incentives to investigation of family life in the period.

However, this was not the only motivation for studying the family. The expansion of interest in this area has been partly due to a growing regard for associated areas such as women's history, childhood and old age, but is also partly the result of increasing anxieties over the survival of the modern family. From the 1950s, there have been frequently voiced concerns about increasing rates of divorce and illegitimacy and their potential for destroying family life as we understand it. These concerns can be seen to have contributed directly to the development of a sociology of the family. Perhaps inevitably, it was not long before historians and sociologists began to search for a longer view of this phenomenon which would help supply answers to modern dilemmas. The development of sociological study also provided tools and issues that historians could attempt to apply to the past. As a result of these factors, the history of the family rapidly expanded and soon began to evolve its own momentum, its own issues and methods of working. Therefore, although the search for the family in the past began with much assumption about what had happened in history, as will become clear, this was to be gradually replaced by a growing body of detailed research, from which a very different (and at the time surprising) picture of family life in the past emerged.

FAMILY OR FAMILIES?

As this area of study has developed as a major force in the discipline of history, those involved in this process have been careful to draw a distinction between the genealogical study of the histories of particular families and the historical study of the family. Present-day social historians, able to rely on hard-won respectability, now generally take a more positive view of genealogical and antiquarian research, and indeed are able to admit their dependence on it for much of their source material and audience. However, this process of creating intellectual distance between 'amateurs' and 'professionals' can be seen as a necessity so that serious study of a topic that, not so long ago, many mainstream historians considered unworthy of attention, could take place. One problem it has created is the assumption in academic circles that there is such a thing as the family: a social organisation that was universal, definable and therefore, very often, measurable. Brief consideration of this issue should make it clear that such an entity is unlikely ever to have existed. Given the social inequalities, regional and local diversity, and demographic conditions in the past, it seems improbable that there could have been a single family experience. With this diversity, in many ways, the genealogist's concentration on individual chains of descent, a reminder of the constant flux in which family life is lived, seems to have much to offer academic study.

The definitions of the family used in the early modern period underline this point. Until the eighteenth century, the term was used to describe a lineage (or line) of decent, wider groups of kin and the household, including any resident servants [28 *pp. 4–5*]. Thus family, kin and household were not separate entities, but overlapping sets. The points at which these definitions met are crucial in understanding the nature of family life in the past, as are the processes by which these definitions became distinct and the term 'family' began to be applied almost exclusively to a married couple and their children.

Perhaps because of these problems, many historians have simply failed to define what they mean by the term 'family'; others who have been aware of this difficulty have often fallen back on the illumination of norms and rules of family life that can be argued to have given it its structure. In fact, most individuals are members of more than one family. The first, into which we are born, known as the family of orientation, not only nurtures us in our infancy, but also determines our place within the social order. A second family is created if an individual establishes his own household. This is the family of procreation, which joins an individual to a new set of relatives and, in the past, was theoretically necessary before children could be brought into the world. This became their family of orientation, which they would leave to continue the process. In the early modern period, the picture was often more complicated than this. With a relatively high rate of mortality, it was unusual for these family structures to survive intact. Family units that were broken by the death of a parent might be reconstructed by re-marriage, sometimes leading to the combination of step-siblings and half-siblings in one household. Moreover, as we will see later, individuals of almost all social ranks very rarely moved straight from the family of orientation to that of procreation. Between these states they often lived and worked within the context of other family groups as lodgers, apprentices and servants, and some historians have argued that they became, in effect, additional members of these units [18 *p. 3*].

Despite these complications, most historians working on these problems in the last forty years have assumed the existence of a family in the past. However, there has been very little consensus on how this entity should be defined. It could be argued that each definition of what the family is has led to a different methodology or approach to investigating family life in the past. Each approach, in turn, has asked different sets of questions and used different sources to attempt to resolve them. In order to understand what early modern family life was like, it is necessary to appreciate these differing approaches, their strengths, weaknesses and conclusions.

Part one of this book, concentrates on these approaches and their findings in an attempt to highlight the ways in which historians have investigated family life in the past and the images it has given us. It also attempts to examine the basic enduring structures of family life with which these approaches have been concerned. The second part attempts to analyse the elements that made up family life at different stages of its developmental cycle, from creation to dissolution, while the final part aims to assess the degree to which family life changed in this period.

APPROACHES AND DEFINITIONS

Part of the work of historians is to impose order on the chaos of historical events and circumstances. They often do so by a process of classification that allows similarities and differences to be understood and highlighted. As with history, so with the work of other historians, whose efforts are often divided into different schools and methodologies. However, no matter how useful these systems of classification are in providing a guide to the published literature, it should not be forgotten that they are only ideas, and not realities set in stone.

In the early years of the modern historical study of the family, with a number of historians breaking new ground, often completely independently, diversity of methods became the rule. In 1980, Michael Anderson achieved something remarkable, by organising these different and diverse efforts into a system of classification, in a work of less than 100 pages [25]. His four approaches were those of *psychohistory*, *demographic studies*, those based on the *sentiments* and, finally, the *household economics* approach.

Although Anderson's system has been highly influential, many historians have objected to his idea of distinct approaches. Peter Laslett prefers to think in terms of emphasis, rather than approach [18]. Ralph Houlbrooke has focused on a variety of influences, including psychology, demography, ideas and sociology, but also law, economics and anthropology [33 *p. 4*]. These are valid points, and there are clearly problems in attempting to classify historians in a simplistic way. However, perhaps a more important issue than the methods chosen by historians, is what their work tells us about their underlying definition of the family, and this is the issue that this section will attempt to highlight.

Anderson's first approach was that of psychohistory, which he dismissed in less than a page. The manifesto of this school of thought is usually seen as a volume edited by Lloyd de Mause in 1974 [51], and its continued influence is evident in the existence of a *Journal of Psychohistory*. This is an attempt to understand individuals in the past by applying the tenants of psychology and psychoanalysis to historical evidence. It is not popular among mainstream social historians because it appears anti-historical. Firstly, the imposition of a system for understanding the mind that originated in the late nineteenth century, and developed in the twentieth, on to people in the pre-industrial past, carries obvious dangers. Secondly, historical sources do not lend themselves well to this form of analysis; historians cannot put their long-dead subjects on the couch and interrogate them in the way contemporary psychiatrists can their patients. Finally, psychology and psychoanalysis are themselves controversial, with many disputing the models they present of the mind or dismissing them as irrelevant. The recent attempts of some historians, such as Lyndal Roper, to use psychology in the context of gender relationships, may herald greater respectability for this approach [232]. Until such respectability is widespread, it is difficult not to consider Anderson's dismissal of this methodology, which treats the family in the past as a mental state, as unavoidable.

The second approach outlined by Anderson was the demographic. In this country, and particularly for the early modern period, this is most closely associated with the *Cambridge Group for the History of Population and Social Structure*. The interests of members of this group, and those influenced by and associated with them, break down into two major areas: historians such as Peter Laslett and Richard Wall have focused on household structure, while Anthony Wrigley and Roger Schofield are among the most eminent of those that have provided a demographic context, using measures of population, fertility and mortality. Both strands have come together in areas such as the study of illegitimacy, age at marriage and family size. This approach tends to rely on 'quantitative' or statistical data, derived from census-type and registration documents, materials including (most obviously) taxation records and parish registers [*Docs 4 and 5*]. It is also an empirical approach, beginning from the premise that certain sources have survived and then attempting to find out what can be determined from them.

This approach has not been without its critics. The quality of the data investigated, the typicality of England and the significance of statistical evidence in evaluating family life have all been called into question. We might add that this also occasionally presents a less than accessible and even tedious solution to the problems of investigating social life in the past. The fundamental concept behind this view can be seen as a definition of the family as a unit of residence and of reproduction.

Anderson's third approach was what he defined as the sentiments, which, as the name suggests, focuses on the emotional content of family life in the past. Members of this group include many pioneers in the history of the family, particularly the cultural and social historians Philippe Ariès and Lawrence Stone, the sociologist Edmund Shorter, and to a lesser extent J. L. Flandrin, R. Trumbach, M. Mitteraur and R. Sieder [184, 55, 54, 28, 56, 35]. Unlike the demographic approach, which is source based, this method originated from issues raised from observations of the modern family or a desire to see the detail of how theories of social change occurred in the past. It has then attempted to find sources that permit those questions and issues to be addressed. Particular areas of interest are the relationships between men and women; parents and children. The means of investigating these relationships have been varied, but include a heavy reliance on 'qualitative data', particularly biographical and literary materials, such as diaries, letters, autobiographies and conduct books [*Docs 1, 2, 3, 11, 14, 15*], although it is worth observing that some, particularly Lawrence Stone, also made considerable use of demographic data. There are obvious problems with this approach. Firstly, that these sources were only generated by a small, and largely male, social elite. Moreover, such materials lend themselves to an anecdotal style of historical writing, which, although often fascinating in the detail it supplies, tells us nothing about the frequency of circumstances or the nature of social change.

Historians working within this approach are most commonly associated with the idea that people in the past did not have the same emotional relationships with members of their families as we assume today. However, this conclusion has been so firmly quashed in recent years that continuity in the nature of family relationships has emerged as the dominant view. Ironically, the historians who have revised this pattern, most obviously Linda Pollock, Ralph Houlbrooke and Rosemary O'Day, have used much the same approach and very similar sources [195, 33, 53]. Where they differ is in the comprehensiveness of their studies, in some cases their willingness to incorporate evidence from other approaches, and the conclusions they have drawn. Advocates of this methodology, whether pessimistic or optimistic about the nature of family relationships in the past, and whether arguing for continuity or change, can all be seen as exploring the family as an idea: a set of shared values or emotions.

Anderson's final methodology was what he termed the 'household economics' approach. He stressed this road to the past as an attempt to deal with some of the problems of the other two major methodologies. He also indicated that, whereas demographics are source based and the sentiments grew out of observations of the contemporary world, this approach arose from a desire to test the theories of social sciences about the family to the past. Among these concepts are those of the life cycle and life course. The argument is that just as individuals undergo a series of stages throughout their life, families are not static, but also have a developmental pattern. Thus, the household is seen not as a social norm, but as a constantly changing and developing unit. Emphasis is on the economic functions of the family, and inheritance as the means by which resources are redistributed. This, then, is the family as a process and economic unit.

Unlike the other approaches he highlights, Anderson offers no sustained critique of household economics, which is perhaps unsurprising given that it is

Anderson's own chosen methodology. We might note that one of its limitations is that it necessitates a form and quality of evidence that is rare before the modern period. It could also be accused of 'economic determinism', an assumption that economic self-interest was the prime motive for social action. The order in which Anderson places his three major approaches is also interesting. If we consider the publication of Ariès's work to be the starting point for the sentiments approach, it predates the earliest products of the most important members of the demographic approach by several years, even in English translation [184]. It could be argued that the sentiments did not gain momentum until the 1970s, with the publication of books by Shorter and Stone, but something similar could be said of the demographic approach [54, 55]. Given that early work on the sentiments has been undermined to such a degree by that of the demographic approach, it seems more logical to assess this group of writers first, and this is the organisation that has been adopted in this book. A sceptic might argue that Anderson used the sentiments as a punctuation mark between the work of demographic historians and that of his own school (which is highly dependent on their endeavours, shares source material and is similar in its use of quantitative analysis), so as to make the distinction clearer.

Anderson does not appear to have found it necessary to significantly revise his system of classification in the recent second edition of his booklet. But perhaps it is necessary to reconsider whether there have been any significant new approaches which have developed in the last decade and a half. I would suggest that another important emphasis is that of anthropological or kinship-based studies. Proponents of this approach include Alan Macfarlane (on whose designation Anderson was interestingly silent), Jack Goody (like Macfarlane, a trained anthropologist), Miranda Chaytor and David Cressy [47, 29, 30, 77, 99].

Because anthropologists deal with societies where the family, in the sense of parents and children, is relatively less important than in the West, they tend to focus on the kinship system as a whole. This separates the fact of biological reproduction from the ideas that structure these relationships, of which the 'family' is one. This is, then, an attempt to adopt an approach to the study of family life in the past that incorporates a broader view of the total system. It is not a method without significant problems. The first is whether it is possible to find materials that allow us to see how individuals and groups in the past related to their more distant kin. The second is the danger that by concentrating on such relationships historians give the impression they were significant, even when the evidence does not support this view. Moreover, this approach cannot be used in isolation, as by its nature it cannot deal with some of the most important issues that surround the more limited family. The study of kinship does, however, present the opportunity to move studies on from a focus on the physical and emotional environments of family life. This approach can be seen as defining the family as part of a wider social and cultural system.

It could be argued that each of these definitions of the family is entirely valid. Each focuses on one vital part of the structure of family life in the past. Only by appreciating the nature of emotional relationships, residence and reproduction, the family life cycle, economics and the kinship system, can we hope to understand the nature of that family life. The remaining chapters in this section will examine each of these differing structures in an attempt to illuminate a framework within which family life can be understood.

CHAPTER TWO

EMOTIONAL LIFE

Was the quality of emotional relationships in the past the same as it is today? This is the question that dominated the historical study of English family life until the 1980s. The answer supplied by most pioneers in the field was that relationships within the family were colder and dependence on those outside much greater. This was, in part, simply because historians expected fundamental social change to have occurred in the early modern period. As we have seen, those who accepted a Marxist model of development saw this era as defined by the transition from feudal, land-bound society, to a more flexible one based on capital and industry. Equally, so-called Whig or liberal historians saw the early modern period as highly significant in the creation of a more individualistic and 'democratic' society in England, which would be ready to take part in an Industrial Revolution from the eighteenth century [21 *p. 3*]. Both sets of changes necessitated a move from an inflexible system based on wider kinship and extensive ties to the rural community, to one founded on the more easily manipulated nuclear family, which, as a result, would have become an isolated, cohesive and affectionate institution. Thus, pioneers in this area of investigation have been associated with two major concepts: firstly, the growth of affection, and, secondly, the development of individualism. Both of these factors play into a third major concept without which they cannot be understood – the rise of the nuclear family.

AFFECTION

The nature of affection has been one of the great areas of debate in the recent study of the early modern family. This controversy can be divided into an examination of relationships between men and women on the one hand, and between adults and children on the other. Changes in these joined areas of interest have been detected in factors such as artistic representations, the nature of courtship, terms of address, advice, the use of corporal punishment, expressions of grief and the commemoration of the dead. Some historians built these factors into a general picture that demonstrated dramatic change, from relatively cold and formal relationships, to those based on genuine affection. However, it is also important to note the very great differences between these historians in their understanding of the timing and stages of these changes.

For Phillipe Ariès, focusing on (but not exclusively concerned with) children, the period of transformation was the sixteenth century, when, he argued, artists began to reflect a new concept of childhood as a distinct state, instead of showing children as merely small adults [184 *pp. 327–52*]. From this, he concluded that childhood, as a concept, was a relatively recent invention. Also concerned with children, L. de Mause's work intensified this picture, arguing for a continual evolution, concluding more extremely that 'the further back in history one goes, the lower the level of child care, and the more likely children are to be killed, abandoned, beaten, terrorised, and sexually abused' [51 *p. 21*]. Shorter's analysis of change in the nature of the family was, he admitted, somewhat undermined by his heavy reliance on evidence from France in the period 1750 to 1850. From this he suggested, but could hardly prove, a widespread and rapid transformation in attitudes to children (particularly between mothers and infants), in sex and in patterns of romantic affection between men and women [54 *pp. 54–78*]. In contrast, Lawrence Stone painted a picture of a staged transformation from the 'open lineage family', dominant in the late medieval era, to the 'restricted patriarchal nuclear family' in the middle of our period, culminating in the 'closed domesticated nuclear family', which was common by the end of the eighteenth century [55]. This he saw as evidenced in increasing expressions of affection for offspring and spouses in conduct books and biographical materials such as diaries and letters. There was also a decline of corporal punishment, and growing grief at their deaths. These developments were paralleled by a renewed emphasis on the morality of marriage, and the development of a literature that created the idea of romantic love and fostered 'companionate marriage'.

All these historians, but especially Stone, relied not only on literary sources, but also on emerging demographic evidence of high mortality, which (as we will see) was particularly concentrated among children. From this, they concluded that individuals would have reacted by withdrawing emotionally from their partners and offspring. In Stone's view there was only a limited amount of 'emotional capital' available for investment and it would not be wasted, particularly on children who might die at any moment [55 *p. 70*]. These arguments, with the implication that ancestors from the seventeenth century and before, were heartless machines, have provided one of the greatest possible spurs to investigations of family life. Partly as a result of this process, this pioneering work has been condemned in almost every possible way.

There are always problems in interpreting art as evidence of social norms, because it may instead reflect skill and convention. Ariès, in particular, has also been criticised for having 'ripped evidence from its proper context'

[33 *p. 6*]. Shorter was very aware of how limited was his evidence for the lack of affection in 'traditional' society [54 *p. 55*]. The greatest difficulty has been that Stone, in particular, argued that there was silence on most matters of affection before the seventeenth century and that this implied a lack of involvement. Given the massive changes that were occurring in the historical record in early modern England, as it moved from an oral, to a written and printing culture, such an argument is obviously flawed. In these circumstances, the more frequent expressions of affection evident in the modern period may simply reflect new forms, and greater quantities, of records.

Such an argument has been rendered irrelevant by the mass of contradictory evidence historians produced in the 1980s: evidence that is remarkably easy to find, even in sources that were well known when these pioneering works were written [*Docs 2 and 3*]. Linda Pollock, focusing on children, has pointed to the genuine affection shown towards them by parents. She indicated that brutality was exceptional rather than common place and that real grief was shown at their deaths, even at the beginning of our period [195]. Similarly, Ralph Houlbrooke, who also examined relations between husbands and wives, concluded that, 'much evidence of love, affection and the bitterness of loss dating from the first half of Stone's period has simply been ignored' [33 *p. 15*].

To give just two examples concerning married love, in 1441 Margaret Paston finished a letter to her husband John by requesting him to wear a ring with the image of St Margaret, 'that I sent you for a remembrance till ye come home' and observing 'ye have left me such a remembrance that maketh me to think upon you both day and night when I would sleep' [2 *p. 5*]. In 1502, Sir Robert Plumpton wrote to his wife Agnes, calling her 'my deare hart', signing his letter, 'your owne lover' and sending it to, 'my entyrely and most hartily beloved wife' [7 *p. 152*].

Finding examples of parental affection is more difficult, largely because people did not write letters to their young children and we have to wait for the diary to emerge as a literary form, as it did towards the end of the sixteenth century. When this occurred, we have examples like that of Lady Anne Clifford, who, when her two-year-old daughter was ill, noted, 'I was fearful of her that I could hardly sleep all night', or more painfully that of William Brownlow who wrote in his diary after the death of his second son, 'I was at ease, but Thou O God has broken mee a sunder and shaken mee to peeces' [195 *pp. 125, 134–5*].

Instances like these suggest that the way in which affection, particularly between men and women, was expressed, was moulded by the terminology of the day, but nevertheless affection was expressed. It therefore appears that, contrary to many assumptions, individuals were unable to suppress their emotions in the calculating way that has often been assumed. Therefore, the warmth of emotion between men, women and children appears to have been very similar to that found in the modern world. However, it seems unlikely that nothing significant changed in this lengthy and volatile period, and we will return to this problem in the final part of this book.

Moreover, there is also a danger of having too rosy a view of early modern family life. If we accept that the emotional range of persons has remained much the same, we must also accept that, even today, many marriages are not loving and not all parents are considerate of their children. No investigation of emotional life would be complete without allowance for the diversity of individual experience.

INDIVIDUALISM

A particularly strong theme in the work of Lawrence Stone was the idea of growing individualism throughout our period. This process has been seen in such diverse elements as patterns of inheritance, choice of marriage partners, developments in the architecture of houses, memorials, family prayers, the pursuit of pleasure, rising illegitimacy and the growth of a pornographic industry in the eighteenth century [55 *pp. 223–69*]. Clearly, if changes in all these areas of society did occur, they would have had profound effects on the nature of family life, perhaps amounting to a watershed in attitudes. The attractiveness of this idea has given it a profound effect on some investigations of the history of the family, and has even left its mark on revisionist work in this area [33, 209].

Stone defined individualism as 'a selfish desire to put one's personal convenience above the needs of society as a whole, or those sub-units of the kin or the family' [55 *p. 224*]. This new ideology was seen as particularly marked in practices connected with the commemoration of the dead. Stone saw the shift from the featureless, stark effigies of the medieval period, surrounded by heraldry, which put them in the context of family and kin, to realistic individual busts and images from the seventeenth century, as indicative of these changes. Similar transformations were occurring in individual portraiture among the social elite. There were also new forms of writing, including the self-revelatory diary and the autobiography, which date from this period. These were part of a literature of self-exploration, which grew to include the novel and the love letter [55 *pp. 224–6*].

Stone argued that these were part of a wider social and political process that was marked in England by growing religious toleration, a recognition of the religious beliefs of the individual and the beginnings of ideas about the ability of man to control and manipulate his environment. He saw the intellectual agents of these ideas to be in the Renaissance idea of Humanism, with its concentration on the individual and his achievements, and in the followers of the Swiss religious reformer Jean Calvin. Calvinists, often linked together with a variety of religious strands in late sixteenth- and early seventeenth-century

England as Puritans, pioneered a religion of introspection with emphasis on the individual's relationship with God, expressed through prayer and Bible reading. This has been contrasted with late medieval Catholicism, which relied heavily on collective and communal rites, such as the Mass [55 *pp. 225, 245, 259*]. We will return to the impact of these ideas on family life in the final section of this book. In Stone's view, these were the engines of change, but the origin of this argument lies in thinking about the nature of property ownership between the late medieval and early industrial periods.

It has long been argued that in the middle ages property was collective, rather than individual, and that the head of a family was no more than the custodian of an estate, which, in effect, belonged to a line or 'lineage'. Thus, the major principle of inheritance was primogeniture, that is to say an estate and headship would normally pass to the eldest male child [55 *p. 87*]. Because the remainder of the family, for example younger brothers and sisters, would be dependent on the head, it was assumed that they would tend to form a large and relatively cohesive family group. It has also been argued that this system was beginning to fragment at the highest levels of society by the seventeenth century, as the influence of family groups gave way to individual preferences. One often-cited example is the choosing of sides in the civil wars, which famously saw families like the Verneys divided between parliament and king [27, 49]. However, even Stone had to accept that primogeniture not only persisted, but was intensified in law in the eighteenth century with the rise of strict settlement. This was a system which helped to keep the estate of a man without sons intact, by entailing it away from daughters towards a single male relative [55 *p. 244*].

The 'rise of individualism' is seen as necessary so that a capitalist economy could flourish from the eighteenth century, a process pioneered in England. In such an economy, property and effort had to be individual, rather than collective, to supply the means and motivation for capitalisation. Thus, even members of conjugal family groups have been seen as more individual, separated by the privacy of separate rooms and increasingly linked by reciprocal roles and responsibilities, rather than each occupying a God-given position in the social order. Here the emphasis placed on the gentry and middling sort by authors contributing to Anderson's sentiments approach, seems justified, as it was among these groups, the future middle classes, that we would expect these elements of family life to have emerged.

The most direct assault on this picture has come from Alan Macfarlane, who argued forcibly that England, at least from the fourteenth century, was already an individualistic society, because property was always held by individuals [90]. What Macfarlane paints is the image of a highly flexible social system already based around personal effort and of which the nuclear family was the primary unit. If this argument is correct, it means that the search for massive, but predictable, shifts in attitudes and actions throughout the early modern period is no longer necessary. As we will see below, this emphasis on continuity interlocks with the evidence brought to light by other historians and it has had a profound impact on our understanding of almost every area of family life in the past.

THE RISE OF THE NUCLEAR FAMILY

The rise of the nuclear or conjugal family, of a couple and their children, and the corresponding fall in the significance of wider kinship and communal bonds, all in the early modern period, has long been a cherished image among sociologists and social theorists. Again, this development has been seen as necessary so that industrialisation could take place. It is also the cross-roads of ideas about growing affection and individualism in the same period, of which the nuclear family is the agent and ideal. This pattern has been perceived in many areas, including the decreasing interference of legal and traditional sanctions, the increasing privacy of the conjugal unit and the rise of domesticity as an ideology [54, 55].

In late medieval England, there was a wide variety of communal and legal sanctions that could be brought to bear on the conduct of sexual and familial behaviour. Manorial courts, often seen as representing the will of the community, were particularly adept at punishing some forms of behaviour, such as scolding and wife-beating [20 *pp. 25–6*]. Similarly, church courts, often acting at the relatively local level of an archdeaconry, were able to punish sexual incontinence and had some control over marriage litigation [144]. Their tendency to be filled with such cases earned them the popular title 'bawdy courts'. It has been noted that in England these institutions began to decline from the sixteenth century. This was in part because the Reformation eroded the powers of the church courts, restricting their sanctions and scope, while there was increasing emphasis on the parish as the smallest unit of local government, rather than the manor. It is therefore argued that the 'community' represented by these institutions was less and less able to interfere in family life and that this resulted in growing autonomy for the conjugal family.

Such an argument is not, however, completely convincing. Firstly, this social control was never applied universally. Historians distinguish between those 'close' nucleated lowland parishes, where social control lay in the hands of one major landholder, or a few landholders, and 'open', dispersed upland or forest parishes, where control of land and society was less concentrated [23 *pp. 171–2*]. Furthermore, although manorial and church courts did decline, they did not do so universally or quickly in the early modern period. For example, the citizens of Acomb, near York, were still appearing before their manorial court to answer to local justice in the nineteenth century [*Doc. 13*]. Church courts were still active, if on a more limited basis, until the same period. It is also true that these institutions could decline, because many of their functions had been taken on by the state. The slow trickle of statutes affecting family life that were passed in this period, such as those against bigamy in 1603, or concerning clandestine marriages in 1753, meant that the state courts took on an increasing role in the regulation of familial and sexual behaviour. By the same process the parish gained considerable powers over the lives of the poor, seen most clearly in the Laws of Settlement which, from the late seventeenth century, were used to regulate whether the poor could marry [157].

If the case of increasing autonomy for the conjugal unit cannot be proved, then what about the possibility of increasing privacy? This has been seen in a number of areas, most obviously in architectural changes, patterns of servant residence, and in activities that promoted the privacy of the body [55 *pp. 256–7*]. Certainly, there were changes in the organisation of the houses of the rich that suggest increasing emphasis on privacy. The open medieval hall, the dominant feature of elite vernacular architecture of the period, where the noble family was 'on display' to their servants and retainers, certainly contrasts with the corridors and privy chambers for dining and sleeping, which became standard in the English country house. It has also been noted that, from the eighteenth century, a number of commentators pointed to a tendency for servants to live 'out', instead of on their master's property. One example is Joseph Brasebridge, who, in the 1770s, bemoaned his lack of control over his apprentice, because he slept at his father's house [55 *p. 255*]. Moreover, there is some statistical evidence that supports this case, with the beginnings of a process that considerably reduced the numbers of servants sharing the households of their masters evident from the mid-eighteenth century [58 *p. 221*]. However, what remains difficult is the relationship of these factors to changing attitudes. As we will see, these developments may have had more to do with alterations in the nature of labour, rather than evolving attitudes to privacy.

The point has been made that even in these new households, the ubiquitous nature of servants meant that the private matters of masters were hardly likely to stay so for long [114 *p. 83*]. Architectural changes can also be read as indicating either contrasting sets of social attitudes towards privacy, or as a radical transformation in the ability of the rich to carry out what they may always have desired, to segregate themselves from the rest of the world. It is also problematic that these patterns (while reflected in an abbreviated form in the houses of yeomen and merchants), like so much of the evidence on which these arguments are based, only extended to a small and wealthy elite. For the majority of the population, it can be argued, as they were forced to lodge in towns or densely packed proto-industrial villages, conjugal privacy did not increase, but decrease.

There is perhaps better evidence for the rise of bodily privacy. As Lawrence Stone noted, it may be more than coincidence that the fork, the handkerchief and the nightdress all came into common usage from the seventeenth century

[*55 p. 256*]. There is also evidence of an increasing desire for privacy in the carrying out of basic bodily functions. Moreover, Puritanism in the late sixteenth and seventeenth centuries has long been associated with a degree of prudery towards the dressing of bodies, even though this view was never dominant. Again, that the inhabitants of early modern England, particularly the rich, had increasing numbers of personal possessions may tell us less about their ideas and priorities and rather more about their developing economy. Certainly, these things changed the quality of many lives, but whether they amounted to a fundamental transformation in the nature of family life is open to debate.

Finally, what of the emergence of domesticity as an ideology in family life towards the end of our period? That eighteenth-century continental comment-ators noted the peculiarly large amount of time English husbands and wives spent together, seems to suggest that domesticity had become a dominant theme. A similar picture can be derived from the internal evidence of diaries, letters and advice to married partners that flourished in this era [162]. How-ever, as with arguments over emotion, the problem here is that, given the change in the volume and nature of source material, we have no means of judging whether this ideology had in fact been predominant in an earlier period. As we will see, comparisons of advice to married couples, from the early six-teenth century onwards, show that there was remarkable consistency in the nature and emphasis on partnership in marriage.

As we will see in the next chapter, one further and fundamental argument against the idea of the rise of the nuclear family, is that there is little evidence that larger extended families ever existed as units of residence. To be fair to the pioneers in this field, they rarely argued that residence was part of this pattern, rather, as Edmund Shorter put it, 'the nuclear family is a state of mind rather than a particular kind of structure or set of household arrangements' [*54 p. 205*]. Nevertheless, this raises the question of whether these perceived changes in behaviour could occur without any apparent effects on household structure. One problem is that the family seen as a state of mind, or set of shared emotional values, is impossible to measure statistically and we are left to debate these factors on a purely anecdotal level.

It appears then that emotional attitudes were remarkably consistent across our period. The investigation of these sentiments has been an important con-tribution to the field, and continues to be so. However, there is a need to separate the study of the emotional aspects of family life from the widely discredited conclusions and assumptions of some of the first historians to examine these issues. Ariès, Shorter and Stone, in particular, have become 'straw men' in debates about family life, and no comment on family or childhood is quite complete without an attack upon them. However, it is possible that this emphasis has been taken too far. There is now perhaps a need to move beyond the debate on emotional life in the past to the wider issues of diversity and adaptation. In recent years, few historians have been willing to rely only on literary and biographical materials to construct a picture of family life, and there is clearly a need to approach the evidence with a greater degree of caution than was evident in the work of some pioneers. An examination of the emotional life of the family in the past still has a significant role in understanding the social world of early modern England, but it is only one possible means of investigating that pattern.

CHAPTER THREE

RESIDENCE AND REPRODUCTION

One obvious means of avoiding the pitfalls inherent in the pursuit of the family through literary sources, is to attempt to press into service the mass of information generated by the early modern English state. This material naturally lends itself to statistical analysis and this inevitably gives such investigations an air of reliability that is lacking in enquiries into the history of the family as a web of intangible emotions. The rise of this form of history owes much to the development of new methods of analysis, originally pioneered in France and highly influential in North America, but which were adapted, refined and pushed forward from the 1950s in Britain. This branch of the history of the family can legitimately claim to be the most successful of all the methodologies employed for the early modern period. Firstly, it placed the study of the family on a scientific basis; secondly, it carried out the most radical transformation of our understanding of family life in the past; and finally, it has remained essential to any investigation of the texture of society in any period. However, as will become clear, these findings have had their critics.

The pioneering work in this arena can be divided into two main areas of interest. Firstly, there is the investigation of the nature of the household and, secondly, the pattern of demographics in the past. Together these factors have produced a picture of the family as a residential and reproductive unit at the centre of social and economic patterns.

RESIDENCE

One of the peculiarities of pioneering historians of English family life, who were researching emotions and demography from the 1950s to the 1970s, was their failure to engage in a direct debate. This was in part because the work of different authors was based on such fundamentally different assumptions. It was implicit in the writing of those investigating the family as an idea or set of emotions, that social mores originated with the elite and then filtered down through the social order. As a result, artistic and literary evidence were perceived as sensitive measures of social change. In contrast, those concerned with residence and reproduction have tended to focus on averages and norms; some would even say its proponents have been obsessed with finding a mythical historical 'everyman'. In these works, where they have been confrontational, and on occasion they have been furiously so, they have tended to attack assumptions that predated the works of Ariès, Stone and Shorter, and to which these historians of the sentiments were indebted (although they may not have known it). In this sense, demographic historians were attempting to pull up the tree by its roots, rather than simply attacking the branches.

For Peter Laslett, the primary targets were ideas about residence formulated by Frederick Le Play, a French engineer turned social commentator, in the nineteenth century. Le Play highlighted three different models of family organisation: the patriarchal family, where large kin groups shared joint ownership of property and land; the stem family, based on co-residence of parents and children and where inheritance was passed down through one child who would remain in the parental home; and finally, the unstable family founded on the conjugal bond, and where parents dispatched children to form new and independent households when they matured. Most importantly, Le Play fashioned these familial forms into an evolutionary model, where primitive societies began with the patriarchal family and moved through the stem family to the unstable family, the characteristic institution of the modern and industrial world [26]. What is most significant for this debate is that each form of family should have had an effect on residential patterns. Therefore, in the pre-industrial period, a change should be evident from large stem families to the smaller, unstable, conjugal or nuclear household. This model was taken up by Marxist historians and widely accepted in liberal circles, because it fitted to a more generally accepted pattern of social change.

What enabled historians to take issue with this scheme is the survival of census-type materials from the early modern period. The first census proper is not available until 1801, but, before that point, the early modern state produced a number of surveys, made for the purposes of taxation, that are very similar in nature. Those that take the form of houselistings, giving the names of members of each household in a parish, and often their relationship to the head of that household, provide a fascinating insight into patterns of residence in the early modern period [*Doc. 4*]. The earliest examined so far is from the 1520s, but there are several from the second half of the sixteenth century and increasing numbers as the period progresses. There are biases in the distribution of parishes by location and type [41, 58]. Nevertheless, they provide a means of investigating just how English households in this period were structured, and therefore of testing assumptions about the nature and evolution of family life.

The increasingly sophisticated investigation of these sources, associated with the *Cambridge Group for the History of Population and Social Structure*, and in particular with the work of Peter Laslett and Richard Wall, is highly complex, but, in summary, demonstrates some vitally important characteristics.

Firstly, it is clear that the Mean Household Size in early modern England was much smaller than was expected by many, at around 4.75 persons overall. The second observation is that kin from beyond the conjugal family (of parents and children) rarely shared residence in these sources, being evident in only around one in ten households. Most damaging for the stem family thesis, was the rare existence of two cohabiting conjugal groups, for example parents and one of their married children. This type of family would have been necessary for the direct transmission of a household between generations. What were evident in 29 per cent of households in 100 pre-1821 communities, were one or more servants, making up some 13 per cent of the general population [58 *pp. 147–9*]. As we will see, the role of servants had a profound effect on the nature of family life in the early modern period. In addition, towards the end of our era there were increasing proportions of households with lodgers and boarders, as high as 20 per cent in some areas.

These findings have not been uncontroversial. In particular, Laslett's expansion of his thesis to suggest that the stem family had never been the predominant form in Europe, brought down the wrath of a number of continental historians. Most acrimoniously, a debate developed between Laslett and Lutz Berkner, who used evidence from Austria in an attempt to prove the existence of the stem family there. Berkner argued that the overall percentage of houses with kin from outside the conjugal family was relatively small; it was most common (60 per cent of cases in his data) where the heads of households were young men, aged 18–27. He used this to argue that household listings present only a 'snapshot' of residential patterns and that it is necessary to examine the family as a process undergoing a life cycle. Thus, relatively few families would exhibit the distinguishing characteristics of the stem family household at any given time, when a youngest or eldest son, his wife and children would share a property with his parents, as this stage took up a short proportion of the life cycle [74, 75]. It has also been argued that very high rates of pre-industrial mortality made households constructed of 'multiple' conjugal couples unlikely and short lived. However, it seems that for England, and possibly even for the rest of Europe, there are insufficient proportions of multiple households to support even this thesis [60]. Nevertheless, Berkner raised a very important point about the nature of the family as a process, rather than a fixed entity. This not only pointed to an alternative way of interpreting the family, but also amounted to a fundamental attack on the definition of the family as a unit of residence, merely a 'household', that lies at the centre of Laslett's work. The problem is that households are measurable; that is why they tend to be used for the purposes of taxation, but families and familial ties are not necessarily identical with the household.

These are not the only criticisms. While the earliest English census that has been examined, from Coventry in 1523, supports the idea that this pattern was long established, the comprehensive nature of census-type materials is less than clear [41]. If there were serious omissions from the evidence, they would tend to be among the poorest social groups, who would have been exempted from taxation. There are also the possibilities of local, regional and social differences. While no clear pattern in the geographical distribution of household types has yet emerged, there were evident differences between communities in Laslett's studies. Clearer still are the social distinctions, with gentry households having a mean household size of 6.63, yeoman farmers of 5.91 and labourers of only 4.51. It remains an open question whether these differences indicate contrasting systems of household composition for different social orders, or whether they were all aspiring to the same system, but some were, for reasons of poverty, unable to fulfil their aim.

However, perhaps the most telling criticism of this method of study, is that it confuses two separate entities: the family and the household, a distinction made most clearly by Rosemary O'Day [53 *pp. 6–10*]. New households were usually formed at marriage, but ties continued to exist to families of orientation. The process of separation was gradual, marked by the death of members of the previous generation and the birth of children to the new couple. Ties of kinship and property continued to exist across the barriers of households. In addition, the household was not simply a sub-set of these ties, as it very often included persons who were not related by any form of kinship, as in the cases of servants and lodgers. Similarly, many servants must have continued to have ties of family to their parents and siblings in other communities and households. The household was not simply the tangible manifestation of the family in early modern England, but a unit of residence that acted as the focal point for different family loyalties.

REPRODUCTION

In exploring the immense potential of evidence for demographic patterns in early modern England, pioneering demographers experienced a steep learning curve, uncovering much that turned upside down assumptions about family life in the past. Many of these assumptions were general, rather than academic, in nature, but the importance of their destruction can hardly be exaggerated. These findings therefore provide a crucial baseline for any serious study of family life.

Such investigations rely heavily on one source, with which England is particularly blessed. The order sent out by Thomas Cromwell in 1538 for the keeping of a register of baptisms, marriages and burials in every parish, meant that England was the first country to provide a nation-wide and continuous record of demographic occurrences, as these rituals approximate to the crucial events of birth, marriage and death. In practice, the record was far less national and continuous than it should have been [17 *pp. 94–111*]. Nevertheless, it provides sufficient information for detailed demographic studies to be undertaken for England from at least the middle of the sixteenth century.

Parish registers have been employed to understand demography in two major ways. The first, aggregative analysis, derives general statistics through calculations based on one or more parish registers. This dates from the early nineteenth century, when John Rickman began to calculate the pattern of population expansion. This process is now carried out with far greater sophistication, and parish registers have been supplemented by the use of other sources, such as marriage licences and census-type materials. However, this method remains limited in the degree to which it allows the reasons for demographic change and its relationship to family life to be understood. The second method, family reconstitution, invented by a French historian Louis Henry, links the separate facts about individual families, to produce a profile of their demographic history. These profiles can then be utilised to provide more detailed data based on the actions and fortunes of these families and their members, including factors such as the size of family groups, the intervals between births and expectations of age at death. However, it is not a method without problems and limitations. For example, only a minority of families, about one-third, can be examined in this way, and these naturally tend to be the least mobile and easiest to trace, often excluding the poorest families [67].

Nevertheless, taken as a whole, these methods illuminate an interesting picture of early modern society. Firstly, they demonstrate that, contrary to many assumptions, in this period marriage was not early, but relatively late, at a mean of around twenty-five or twenty-six years for women and twenty-six to twenty-eight years for men (which compares with ages of twenty-two and twenty-four, respectively, in the 1970s) [73 *p. 255*]. Child marriages may have endured among some members of the nobility and in some areas, such as Lancashire and Cheshire, but they appear to have been highly exceptional [109]. Also somewhat contrary to expectations, women did not have large numbers of children in quick succession, with gaps of two to three years being common. Late marriage, and long intervals between births, meant that completed families did not tend to be large, with a mean of six to seven children born to each family. Moreover, illegitimacy was relatively infrequent in the early modern period; extra-marital births remained below 3 per cent of the total for every decade between the 1540s and 1750 (except in the crisis years of the 1590s, which saw widespread poverty and starvation). In the nineteenth century, it would reach twice that proportion [18 *p. 159*]. Thus before the mid-eighteenth century, marriage and the fact that relatively high proportions of women remained unmarried, would have had profound effects on rates of reproduction [68 *pp. 2–20*].

In other respects, what was assumed about family life has been confirmed. Mean life expectation was relatively low in the pre-industrial period, being in the early forties at birth [73 *p. 252*]. Rates of mortality were particularly high among children, with around a quarter dying before the age of ten and more than half of these in the first year of life. By the same token, once maturity had been reached, adults could anticipate a relatively long life – a mean of another thirty years [73 *p. 250*]. These circumstances inevitably had profound effects on the nature of family life and, as we will see, they fundamentally affected the shape of the family life cycle and behaviour of individuals.

The data derived from both parish registers and household listings has been attacked for its potential inaccuracy and its lack of typicality, as well as some of the conclusions drawn from the data [66]. Anglican parish registers are inherently problematic as sources. It cannot be emphasised enough that they do not record births, marriages and deaths, but baptisms, marriages and burials. They often contain gaps before 1601 and are, unusually, increasingly inaccurate as the period progresses. This is because greater numbers of Protestant non-conformists, Catholics and those who simply avoided religion altogether, chose to disregard these Anglican rites, or postponed them, sometimes indefinitely. Despite the best attempts to estimate this shortfall, all statistics derived from them can only be an indication of events. Moreover, the 404 parishes used by Wrigley and Schofield in their study of the population history of England, often determined by the presence within them of a willing volunteer, have been criticised for their lack of representativeness of the county as a whole [73]. More fundamentally, the tendency to reduce complex statistical evidence to an average prompted Jean Flandrin to describe it as the production of a 'meaningless mean', a figure that tells us little about the actual experience of family life [28 *pp. 53–6*].

However, such criticisms tend to disregard the very careful nature of this work and the open admission that it represents a best estimate, rather than a set of definite facts. While Wrigley and Schofield's *magnum opus* may discourage valid criticism because of its pure weight of scholarship, its careful explanation of methodology makes all too apparent the authors' awareness of the problems they faced [73]. Despite these limitations, although the meaning of, and conclusions drawn from this form of study will remain open to debate, it cannot be denied that it has provided a framework for understanding family life that is unlikely to be seriously challenged in the near future.

THE FAMILY AND POPULATION

Stress on the continuity of household forms and indications of demographic circumstances in the early modern period, can give the impression of a society deep frozen for over three centuries. The most obvious antidote to this danger is that, as we have already seen, across our period the population of England increased by approximately a factor of three. Additionally, there were fluctuations in almost all the statistics cited above during the period, some of considerable magnitude and importance. For example, the illegitimacy ratio fell from around 3 to 4 per cent in the 1540s to its 'nadir', in the 1650s of around 1 per cent, before it began its steady rise and passed 4 per cent by the end of our period [65 *pp. 176–91*]. It has been suggested that this was due to variations in the emphasis on social control exercised by Puritan elites, which grew towards the middle of the seventeenth century, but declined after the Restoration in 1660 [83]. Confusingly, it has also been argued that the relative size of age groups present in the population changed significantly over time, and this may, in part, explain changes in these rates, as the young are more likely to engage in illicit sexual activity [69 *p. 42*]. However, Peter Laslett pointed to the relationship between this figure and the mean age at marriage, for both men and women, which rose and fell in almost inverse proportion [18 *p. 161*]. We might expect circumstances where marriage became more difficult (and therefore occurred later) to result in more illegitimate births among frustrated potential brides and bridegrooms. But it seems that, in early modern England, the same factors that repressed marriage acted successfully to repress illicit sexual activity.

As this example indicates, while one important role of demographic historians has been to illuminate the basic circumstances of life in the past, a more significant and difficult undertaking is to explain these circumstances and the relationships between them. We will return to the theme of demographic change and the family in the final section of this book, but at this point it is important to attempt to understand how the major elements of this picture fitted together, particularly the way in which the household related to the pattern of early modern demography.

When Thomas Malthus founded the modern science of demography in the late eighteenth century, he placed the emphasis on the effects of mortality. Put very simply, his argument was that population growth was checked by the impact of famine or disease, which would keep it within its natural resource base. Modern demographers, while acknowledging their debt to Malthus, have increasingly come to see fertility as a more significant factor [27 *pp. 4–8*]. Although a crisis, like the famines of the late 1590s or the outbreak of plague in the 1660s, might appear to have a profound effect on the size of a population, these losses tended to be rapidly made up. This was partly because the death of adults led to earlier inheritance and the availability of more resources, such as farms or businesses, which allowed a younger generation to marry earlier than would otherwise have been the case. For example, after the epidemic of 1725–29 in Worcestershire, there was a surge of marriages, followed by a mini-'baby boom' of baptisms over the next five year. In another twenty-five to thirty years there was an echo of more marriages and baptisms as the next generation reached maturity [62 *pp. 403–9*].

As we have already seen, the overwhelming majority of births in early modern England occurred within the context of marriage, meaning that this relationship was the major factor in determining fertility. This was the institution around which new households were created, and so limitations on household creation, and on conception within them, were vital in this process. Put in another way, the household was at the centre of the demographic system in early modern England and changes in its construction and nature would have had profound effects on the general pattern of life.

In this process, changes in other factors also become highly significant. Firstly, the proportion of the population never marrying fell in the last century of our period. In the decades around 1700, roughly a quarter of people aged forty to forty-four had not married, but a century later it was only between one in ten and one in twenty of the population [73 *p. 260*]. Similarly, age at marriage was tending to fall. Brides at their first marriage, who were a mean age of 26.5 in twelve parishes in the period 1650–99, were followed by a cohort aged a mean of only 24.9 in the period 1750–99 [71, 73 *pp. 257–65*]. The result of these two factors was that a larger proportion of the population were able to have children at an earlier age, and this goes some considerable distance towards explaining the rapid population growth that was beginning at the end of the eighteenth century.

Malthus was the first to link this situation to movements in prices and wages. He argued that population expansion would tend to create food short-ages, which would in turn increase prices, depress the value of real wages and mean that marriage would tend to be late. In turn, when the population eventually began to fall as a result of these circumstances, the reverse would occur, with less demand for resources raising the real value of wages and leading to earlier marriage and increased population. This model fits well until the late eighteenth century, ironically the time when Malthus made this obser-vation, but from this point, the connection appears to have been broken, with prices continuing to fall and wages increasing in value despite population growth. Wrigley and Schofield argue that this was because there was a genera-tion time lag between the effects of economic change and family behaviour [73 *pp. 306–8*]. Another explanation, as we will see, is that the link between resources and marriage was broken by changes in the economic and social structure.

It is obvious that the role of the household and the pattern of demo-graphic change in early modern England are connected in extremely complex ways. It is difficult to understand these interactions by investigating the gen-eral patterns and trends in demography in isolation. In part, the work of other historians, particularly those of what Anderson termed the household economics approach, has been an attempt to understand these connections through a focus on the household as an economic unit, to investigate how it was constructed, how it functioned, reproduced and was dissolved.

The examination of the family as a unit of residence and reproduction, has made extremely good use of the wealth of information available, to produce an important (if not incontrovertible) framework, within which we can under-stand family life in the past. While these findings have stressed the continuity of fundamental familial forms, this should not be confused with the changes that could and did occur within the context of this framework. However, a number of limitations in this definition of the family have been highlighted and it is clear that, in itself, demographics is insufficient as a means of investigating and understanding the totality of family life in the past.

CHAPTER FOUR

LIFE CYCLE AND ECONOMY

One of the most significant contributions to our understanding of family life is the awareness that families are not fixed entities, but the results of systems of social organisation. These ideas originated in sociology and social theory, but have an obvious applicability to the work of historians, who have the potential to investigate these processes in the context of change across time. The emphasis on economics has been part of an attempt to shift investigations away from the broad, 'macro', picture of agricultural methods, manufacture and trade, to an attempt to understand how the family functioned as an economic unit at the 'micro' level. These areas can only be understood in relation to each other; accordingly, this chapter will first attempt to outline the pattern of the family life cycle, before turning to the ways in which resources were redistributed between families and how they were utilised to maintain the family unit.

LIFE COURSE AND LIFE CYCLE

Although historians often use the term 'life cycle' to describe the changing roles of an individual, it has been pointed out that there is nothing circular about the pattern of human life as it runs its course from birth to death. Rather, this term is most appropriate for families which do undergo a process of development and renewal. The distinction between the life course of the individual and the life cycle of the family is an important one, as it shifts the focus from the changing roles of individuals to their part within a more complex and enduring structure. The nature of this process is vital in understanding how family life functioned in the past, the impact of demographic circumstances, and the role of social expectations [76, 80, 81, 82].

The types of sources that have been particularly useful for the study of the life cycle in early modern England, are very similar to those used in the pursuit of demographic evidence. Most important have been records of residence, like houselistings, but also other taxation documents, such as those for subsidies and the hearth taxes of the mid- to late-seventeenth century, particularly where there are several listings that allow change over time to be understood [*Doc. 6(a)–(c)*]. Also important are records that deal with points of transition between different stages in the life cycle, most obviously parish registers, but also court records that provide details about these events. Finally, probate documents, such as wills and inventories of goods, present an opportunity to see the nature of relationships and the transmission of property when death threatened to change the shape of family life [*Doc. 7*].

The pattern these sources illuminate can be divided into two parts; the rules and norms that gave the family system its shape, and the effects of these rules. Of these, the rules behind the system are extremely simple and straightforward. Firstly, most individuals left home when relatively young, usually to act as servants or apprentices and, secondly, it appears to have been accepted that two conjugal couples should not share a household.

These rules can be inferred from literary sources. For example, the account of one Italian visitor of the fifteenth century noted of English parents' actions towards their children that 'having kept them at home till they arrive at the age of seven or nine years at the upmost, they put them out, both males and females, to hard service in the houses of other people' [184 *p. 353*]. Similarly, in the early seventeenth century William Whately advised prospective husbands when they married, 'if it may be, live of thyself with thy wife, in a family of thine own' [23 *p. 69*]. To these examples we can add the weight of evidence from household studies demonstrating that these patterns appear to have been widely adhered to.

The consequences of these rules were considerable. The concept of service for the young meant that many parents shared their houses with their own children for only a few years. It explains why there were large numbers of households with resident servants. It has been noted that, in a statistical sense, servants acted as a substitute for children [58 *p. 58*]. This, in turn, broke the links between the child and the family of orientation at a relatively early point. It also often severed the connection with the community of origin and may in part explain the much noted and surprisingly high, geographical mobility of early modern English society, where it was rare for individuals to be born and die in the same parish. That couples desired to establish a new and separate household from their parents had a limiting effect on prospects for marriage. Partners could only marry after a period of hard work and hard saving, often while in service. The result was the relatively late marriage pattern we have already seen, and which was shared across north-western Europe.

Children were also often dependent on their parents reallocating some of their resources so that they might marry. Often this was through 'portions', a share of the parents' wealth given over at marriage or maturity. Furthermore, it is probably no coincidence that the mean age of marriage, in the mid- to late-twenties, was close to the mean point at which parents would have been dying, in their late fifties and early sixties. This was when their resources would be passed down to their heirs. However, we should perhaps not envisage frustrated betrothed couples waiting for long periods, vulture like, for their parents to die before they could marry. Instead, there usually seems to have been a gradual process, by which parents redistributed their resources among their children as they began to mature, culminating, on occasion, in a form of retirement or in death. But the resources of one set of parents would normally be insufficient for all their children. This was part of the reason that service and training were so important; they were processes by which parents attempted to secure the future of the next generation. The members of this generation were expected to produce a return, either in skills, employment or capital, so that they could be self-supporting.

Although these social rules have been presented here as if they were absolute, there were, of course, many exceptions. These were most common at the top and bottom of the social order. The rich naturally tended to have larger households and more capital. Therefore, it was easier for them to share houses between conjugal couples and to establish children with an income at an earlier point in their lives. As a result, earlier marriage and complex households were more common among the gentry and nobility [58 *p. 154*]. Similarly, at the bottom of society, the poor would perhaps never own land and tended to rely on pay in exchange for their labour. As a result, they would be at the peak of their earning power while young and fit and had an incentive to marry and have children earlier. This, then, was a pattern that frayed at the edges of the social tapestry. The life cycle of early modern English families was also frequently incomplete. With high mortality and low fertility, it was not uncommon for this process to be curtailed or terminated, due to the death of a partner or a lack of children.

However, if these circumstances did not arise, the pattern is fairly clear. Individuals tended to leave home early and enter another household or series of households. New families were then formed when they reached maturity and set up their own households. This might be shared with servants, and their children were likely to leave when relatively young. The couple then began to undergo a process by which they dismantled their resources and redistributed them to their children. This might be gradual; it could also be sudden if they died or retired.

This pattern raises a number of interesting questions concerning the nature and effect of these stages upon family life in early modern England, and it is to these issues that we will turn in the second part of this book. A further set of issues, highlighted by the exceptions to these rules, concerns the degree to which different social groups and individuals were operating within one family system, and these will form the emphasis of the next chapter. Finally, there is the question of how these units of resource, the families created by this system, functioned and redistributed their assets.

RESOURCES AND INHERITANCE

The resources available to a family included not only the obvious elements, such as money, land, livestock and goods, but can also be seen in terms of customary rights and the skills or abilities of members of the family group. Money, in the form of coins, was increasingly significant throughout the period, but it seems likely that large quantities were rarely amassed. Instead, wealth tended to be tied up in investments, loans, items of value like silver plate, and the resource on which there has been the greatest emphasis, land [47]. In many ways, this concentration is entirely justified. Land, in a largely agricultural economy, was the largest area of production. It was also the most obvious area for investment and carried implications of status. For this reason, it was not uncommon for successful urban businessmen to crown their careers by buying a country estate and attempting to acquire the title of gentleman. However, land ownership came in many forms, from copyhold, in effect a form of rent, to freehold, where the land was virtually owned outright. As we move down the social scale the limited ownership of even small quantities of land could be vital in the economics of the family. Thus the redistribution of resources, and especially land, were crucial to the continued viability of the family unit.

Inheritance has assumed a central role in understanding this process because it appears to present a mechanism for the redistribution of resources between one generation and the next. In some ways, this impression is unfortunate, because the main source for the study of inheritance, wills, does not deal with all of an individual's property, but only what they decided, or remembered, to allocate. This problem can be compensated for, to a degree, by the use of inventories (made of the deceased's goods and assets by his or her neighbours after his or her death) and by the use of probate accounts (that detail the process of distribution) [94, 86]. However, two major problems remain. Firstly, most wills were made only when inheritance was not straightforward, most commonly when an adult was leaving children who were minors or where there was no clear heir; therefore they represent not a normal, but an unusual pattern of resource distribution [91]. Secondly, probate dealt only with the distribution of resources after death, and it seems unlikely that this was the sole point at which this process occurred. Where full records survive they indicate that land, and other items, were passed on, sold and resold with bewildering frequency. Again this can be compensated for by the use of other documents, such as household accounts, manorial rolls and surveys, but these tend to be confined to the relatively wealthy or deal only with the transfer of land. Arguably, at the base of society, where crucial resources might be relatively small sums of money, or even items such as cutlery and crockery, the picture of how this process was carried out remains unclear. Nevertheless, within these considerable limitations, the study of inheritance does demonstrate some interesting aspects of the processes by which families were maintained when early death threatened to destroy them, and by which resources were redistributed when they were dissolved.

It is necessary to understand that inheritance did not operate within a single legal system. While most aspects of probate were the concern of the Church through its courts, throughout our period, inheritance itself was governed by the common law of the kingdom. Neither of these systems was uniform. The law of probate varied between the two historic archdioceses of the country, that of Canterbury in the South and most of the Midlands and of York in Nottinghamshire and the North. The practice of inheritance also varied according to local custom. The city of London functioned on its own principles, while across the county, but most obviously in Kent (where the custom of 'gavelkind' determined how estates should be partitioned), there were tiny pockets governed by local practice [36].

It has generally been assumed that these jurisdictions had profound effects on the nature of inheritance and thus of landholding and family life. A particular distinction has been drawn between areas where the 'rival' customs of primogeniture and unigeniture were dominant [255, *pp. 9–12*]. Under primogeniture, which applied in most areas, an estate would normally pass to an eldest son and his descendants, after him to his brothers and their descendants and only then to any daughters and their offspring. In contrast, systems of unigeniture, or partible inheritance, like gavelkind, would divide an estate between sons and/or daughters. In theory, primogeniture should result in larger estates and impoverished junior branches of families. Unigeniture should have resulted in a more fragmented pattern of uniform, but smaller, holdings. Oddly enough, despite the many assumptions that have been built upon these contrasts, few historians have managed to prove that such variations actually manifested themselves in practical terms.

One reason for this is undoubtedly the phenomenon we have already observed, by which parents of the landholding orders were careful to plan for their children's futures, by ensuring that they received training, and by investing their estates in them. It was when this process was not well advanced, often because high mortality took fathers away when families were relatively young, that probate could be used to set up a pattern that would ensure a similar distribution of resources. Usually sons, and particularly eldest sons, were favoured in this process, but a desire to secure the future of all children, male and female, older and younger, is frequently evident [44]. Probate was often about circumventing some of the problems of both types of custom: securing the futures of younger children and daughters where primogeniture predominated and attempting to preserve the viability of family holdings for main beneficiaries where unigeniture affected the landed social orders. Therefore, rather than stressing the significance of different inheritance patterns, what seems to have been more important was the universality of assumptions about family life that helped maintain similar results despite legal variations.

The concentration on landholding is also often deceptive, as land did not necessarily have to be owned to be used. This is particularly true in parts of the North and West, where there were large areas of fell, moor, woodland and heath, on which local inhabitants could graze their animals [255 *p. 9*]. As a result, the ownership of cattle and sheep assumed a much greater significance in the economic world of individual families. A similar effect was created by large areas of fen and marsh, which were most common in the East of the country and which could be farmed by locals for resources such as rushes and wildfowl. Finally, in coastal areas, ownership of fishing vessels permitted harvesting of the resources offered by the sea. These were not the only rights that helped ensure survival. Customs that allowed the picking of wood, or gleaning of fallen corn in harvest, all helped to supplement the resources of the poor and to ensure their survival. However, there is considerable evidence that growing population tended to reduce the viability of these resources as they were shared among increasing numbers and this may in part explain the development of formal systems of charity from the sixteenth century.

There were also attempts to limit these rights by local elites, most obviously where they concerned hunting, but also through enclosure. This probably reflects a better documented stage in a process that dates back into the medieval period; however, such attempts may have been enjoying increased success, limiting the options of the poor and bringing them in contact with the system of criminal law [20 *pp. 123–31*]. Finally, although agriculture predominated, it was not the only form of economic activity. Thus skills, such as metalworking or the ability to write, could be put to advantage. As we have already seen, many of these skills took a considerable period to acquire. Moreover, they were often of little use without certain equipment, such as a forge and tools, which were often specifically mentioned in wills and inventories.

In summary, the members of a household could rely on a complex set of resources, many of which are hard to perceive in the surviving records, but which were vital to the economic viability of every family. While land was the most important, other assets could be highly significant, particular on the lower rungs of the social ladder. Patterns of inheritance reflected these concerns and suggest common assumptions about family life and similar aims in very different circumstances. Most importantly, they point to the possible impact of social and economic factors on family life in general, circumstances that can be seen in the economic roles of individuals within the household.

ECONOMIC ROLES

In order to understand how resources were utilised, it is necessary to investigate the balance that was struck between production and consumption. This can be seen as highly influenced by the structure of the household, which, of course, was subject to change throughout its life cycle. It can also be seen in the roles undertaken by the different members of that household and how they acted as units of consumption and production.

The most obvious place to begin is with the position of the legal head of the household, the husband and father. Although the earning ability of men differed considerably across society, there can be little doubt that the primary economic responsibility, and (it must be said) power, was theirs. As we have already seen, this could be expressed in a number of ways. Among the social elite, income could be generated by investment and from estates. Lower down it was earned from skills, some professional, as among lawyers, others that were crafts, such as carpentry and metalworking. They might also work alone or with others on their own agricultural land, or utilise local rights such as over grazing. Finally, those without access to these resources, or where they proved insufficient, might sell their labour, either in a manufacturing process or, more commonly, as an unskilled agricultural worker. The contrasts between these different resources and the social groups that were associated with them would have had a considerable impact on the productivity of a household across the life cycle.

The evidence suggests that, even in times of relative economic prosperity, the wages earned by labourers were not sufficient to sustain a household for long. The most obvious means of supplementing this income was through the work of other members of the household and therefore marriage opened up greater possibilities for generating income. This theme has been a subject of interest since 1919 when Alice Clark published her study of the working life of women in the seventeenth century [239]. She identified many of the trades undertaken by women; a number were common among housewives, including particularly spinning, tailoring, inn-keeping and brewing. Women, although excluded from many crafts and gilds, were usually able to keep the rights earned by their husbands if they were widowed and thus could often run an existing business as they might a farm or even a large estate. Unmarried women might undertake many similar tasks to the married and they also held a virtual monopoly at the beginning of our period over medicine, nursing and midwifery. However, these were often not jobs of high status, as they often are now, but one of the few options left to women who found themselves on the economic margins. The wives of those who held land also often undertook agricultural tasks, particularly in periods when the demand for labour was heavy, most obviously in ploughing or at harvest, when the men would reap corn and the women stack and glean.

Women also had to intersperse these income-generating activities with a considerable number of household chores. Thomas Tusser's *Five Hundred Points of Good Husbandry*, published in 1580, gives an indication of the 'ideal'. Housewives should rise at four or five o'clock, depending on the time of year. They should prepare breakfast and dinner, clean floors, do laundry, bake, but also feed cattle and milk cows, brew, card and spin wool. In the afternoon, they should sew, fill pillows, and make candles. In the evening they would bring in the washing, feed hens and pigs, then lock up the animals and the house, serve supper, wash up and amuse their husbands before retiring at nine or ten o'clock [1 *pp. 198–203*]. What evidence we have suggests this was not a completely unrealistic pattern. However, it varied a great deal depending on circumstance. Wealth diminished the hard labour and the wives of a substantial proportion of the population would have spent much of their time directing servants in these tasks. Wealth also reduced the need for self-sufficiency as items such as candles could have been bought, particularly in towns. It has also been pointed out that the very poor were saved much cleaning and laundry because they had less to maintain [132 *pp. 109–10*]. Nevertheless, women's work patterns show an important mixture of duties crucial to the maintenance of a household, contributing to the agricultural output of the farm or smallholding and utilising skills and labour that would bring in important income.

It is also necessary to note that men and women were not the only members of a household that could be economically productive. Although children were clearly a burden when very young, they could take part in economic activities from a relatively early age. For example, children as young as six or seven could learn to card wool so that it could be spun. Girls appear to have helped their mothers with quilting and button-making from a similar age and the accidents in medieval coroners' rolls indicate that boys followed their fathers in their daily agricultural round from a relatively early age, suggesting that they emulated and helped them where possible [32 *pp. 183–4*]. However, what is uncertain is the degree to which these economic contributions to the household began to outweigh the costs that extra mouths created. It is clear that productivity increased with age, but the existence of life cycle service, although not entirely determined by economics, in itself suggests that greater productivity was likely outside, rather than inside, most households.

In the majority of cases, men undertook the most important role in the production of resources. However, women and children could be significant in this process. These trends were likely to be more marked where high mortality or a lack of marriage prospects created households led by, or consisting only of, women. They were also more common lower down the social scale, where economic necessity meant that the gap between production and consumption of resources was likely to be much narrower and the need to increase production that much greater. As we will see in the final part of this book, these were circumstances that were proving increasingly common through the early modern period. It is also worth considering the impact these different economic circumstances and the roles of members of the household would have had on their social roles and their relationships to each other.

The concept of the life cycle not only provides a vital contribution to our understanding of the connections of households and families to economic and social circumstances in the past, but it also furnishes us with a useful tool for examining the nature of family life, from formation to dissolution. This pattern will form the basis of the second part of this book, but before that, in the final chapter of this section, it is necessary to investigate how these factors were connected through the wider system of relationships known as kinship.

CHAPTER FIVE

KINSHIP

While historians of the household economics approach have been most influenced by sociology and social theory, those investigating kinship tend to look to ideas originating in social anthropology. Anthropologists, researching other contemporary societies with very different systems for organising family life, are unable to make the same assumptions about the existence of 'the family' that sociologists and many historians have done. Therefore, they have tended to be less interested in the emotional quality of relationships between men and women, or parents and children. Nor have they been as concerned with residence like demographic historians. There is most common ground between this area of study and that of household economics, because of a similar emphasis on process and change over the life cycle. But this methodology has a wider brief, tending to look not at the family, but at the kinship system as a whole. Additionally, the major debate in this area has been over the nature and significance of relationships with wider kin. What this debate helps to illuminate is the way in which different circumstances affected the use of kin and the kinship system.

THE KINSHIP SYSTEM

There is widespread agreement that the form of the kinship system in pre-industrial England was (as it is today), in anthropological terminology, 'ego-centred' – that is to say, it was focused on individuals, not groups. Each individual had a unique set of kin and described them by a distinct set of terms, such as father, brother, uncle and cousin. This contrasts with many systems used in other societies, where kin and terminology are defined by groups and generations of descent. The English kinship system was also bi-lateral – that is to say, descent was counted from both parents, as opposed to patrilineal and matrilineal systems where it is only inherited from a father or a mother. Descent through the male line was easier to trace because surnames (from the fourteenth century) were passed down patrilineally, but heraldry and genealogy indicate that, at least among the social elite, track was kept of both lines. As a result of this system, we have to see every individual in early modern England at the centre of a large network of kinship. This stretched back through the generations of their ancestors, the roots of the family tree, and down through their descendants, who spread out like the branches, an image often used in early modern artistic representations of the family [105].

However, the system was even more complex than this. As in most societies, kin in early modern England existed in three broad categories. The most important were those related, in the language of the day, 'by blood' (referred to by anthropologists as consanguinial or cognatic kin), that is, those to whom one has a biological relationship; for example, fathers, mothers, siblings and children, and all ancestors and descendants. The next most important group were kin related through law or custom (known as affinal or agnatic kin); this includes spouses, parents-in-law, children-in-law and step-relatives. Finally, anthropologists distinguish a third form of kinship which existed in pre-industrial England, that of fictive, ritual or spiritual kin. These were created through a ceremony and mirrored other forms of kinship, rather like the famous example of blood-brotherhood. In pre-industrial England, this included two major relationships, those created at baptism between godparents, godchildren and co-parents and those created at confirmation between the person being confirmed and his or her sponsor [98].

Anthropologists often place considerable stress on the terms used to describe kin and something of the nature of the English system can be seen reflected in the language used. The unique nature of each individual's kinship network can be perceived in these terms, which were all descriptions of the relationship seen from their perspective. The bi-lateral nature of descent can be seen in the unusual habit of using the same terms to describe kin on the father's and mother's sides of the family, most obviously for uncles and aunts. The distinction between consanguinial and affinal kin was drawn by adding suffixes, such as 'in-law'. Today prefixes are used to distinguish different forms of affinal kinship, such as step-brother or half-sister, but, interestingly, in early modern England, these terms were rarely used and almost all such relationships were 'in-laws', if they were distinguished at all. This may indicate that there was actually less precision in the use of language to describe kin than is common today and this may be taken to suggest that the precise nature of relationships was relatively unimportant. Similarly, unlike many societies, once we move beyond a small group for whom there were specific terms, we soon reach a circle of kin usually simply referred to as 'cousins' or simply as 'kinsfolk'. Although early modern writers sometimes distinguished their first cousins 'germain', they rarely used the numbering system, common now, of 'first', 'second', 'third cousins', or identified the line of descent by stating that they were 'once', 'twice' or 'three times removed'. This has often been taken to indicate that individuals in early modern England were rather vague about their relationships and that kinship was therefore relatively unimportant. However, it is worth pointing out that one of the problems of the English kinship system is its extreme complexity. For a relationship to be understood, every link in the kinship chain has to be known. This also meant that individuals had, potentially, a very large number of kin, which made them difficult to describe.

Although the potential network of kin was enormous, sociologists distinguish different varieties of kin. There tends to be a smaller group that are 'recognised', which is to say those with whom the links of kinship are acknowledged and known by an individual. Within this is a smaller circle who are 'affective', that is to say with whom the individual has some sort of practical relationship. Finally, within this is the inner-circle of 'intimate' kin, with whom they identify their interests and share their resources and daily life. The debate, then, is over where the inhabitants of early modern England drew these concentric circles within the wider kinship network.

In many societies, one of the major functions of a kinship system is to create a circle within which marriage was not possible, because it was considered to be incest. In late medieval canon (church) law this circle was very wide. Prohibited kin included consanguinial or affinal relatives to the fourth degree (that is the descendent of an individual's, or his or her spouse's, great-great-grandparents). What is more, illicit affinity (created by sex outside marriage) and godparenthood both created prohibitions to the second degree [*28 p. 19*]. These prohibitions were not merely formalities and were backed up by the church courts. For example, in 1463 John Hawthorne of Tunbridge in Kent was sentenced to be whipped three times round the church and market for the crime of marrying his deceased wife's goddaughter.

It has been calculated, on the conservative assumption that each of an individual's relatives had one descendent of each sex, that a person would be unable to marry a staggering 188 kinsfolk [*28 p. 27*]. However, only eighty-eight of these would have been of the same generation and only half of these of the opposite sex, leaving forty-four individuals, still a considerable number, who could not have been legal marriage partners and excluding those created by illicit sex, baptism or confirmation.

Henry VIII's marital difficulties and the break with Rome in the 1530s, led to changes in this system. Henry needed to modify the law on marriage to justify his divorce from Catherine of Aragon and later to allow him to marry his cousin through marriage, Catherine Howard. As a result, the ultimate authority became the prohibitions contained in Leviticus chapter 18. However, these were in many ways inadequate and needed clarification. Due in part to the many changes of regime in the sixteenth century, this was slow in coming. Although Archbishop Parker put forward his 'Tables of Kindred and Affinity' in 1563, they were not formally made binding until 1603 [*Doc. 8*]. They were publicised by being placed in parish churches and in the back of the Book of Common Prayer from 1681, but it is clear that there was considerable confusion over, or wilful ignorance of, their contents [29 *pp. 178–81*]. They limited the barriers of marriage to an individual and his or her children, siblings, nephews, nieces, step-children, uncles, aunts and grandparents. But they were not clear on whether an individual could marry his or her siblings-in-law and did not include first cousins, which many felt they should. Illicit affinity was treated like marriage and the restrictions on marrying relations through godparenthood were removed [105 *pp. 23–7*].

The question must be raised as to whether all this made any difference to people's relationships with their kin. The answer is that it probably did only on very rare occasions. Even in the medieval period, the seemingly cumbersome restrictions on marriage could be disregarded for a fee by purchasing a dispensation from the Church. Dispensations to marry closer kin were rarely granted and probably rarely requested, implying that in practice, the changes in the law merely shrank the marriage prohibitions to approximately where society felt they should be. It seems most people thought that relatives who shared a grandparent should be included, but beyond that, they were relatively unconcerned. If so, it seems that the circle of recognition of kin in early modern England was relatively small compared with many non-European societies.

RELATIONSHIPS WITH DISTANT KIN

If kin recognition was limited, then what determined the shape of affective relationships and intimacy with kin? The nature of these connections has been the central debate in this field over recent years. Part of the criticism of the work of Stone and Shorter was their apparent assumption that, at the beginning of our period, kin were highly significant in family life. Stone saw the rise of the nuclear family at the expense of kinship and political clientage among the aristocracy, while Shorter described the nuclear family coming to 'prefer friendship with close kin to interaction with the concentric rings of uncles and aunts . . .' [55 *pp. 123–9*, 54 *p. 4*].

The starting point for objections to this pattern of change is the detailed investigations of household structure that we possess, which indicate that they rarely included other kin outside the conjugal family. In the forty-six listings that recorded kin between 1574 and 1821, from Peter Laslett's sample of 100 English communities, only around one in ten households contained additional resident kin [58 *p. 149*]. What is more, since these amounted to only 946 persons in 626 households, clearly in most cases there were only one or two additional kin present. This evidence largely destroys any residual image of the pre-industrial family as a large collection of grandparents, aunts, uncles and cousins all living under one roof. The specific relationship between these persons is only known in roughly two-thirds of these cases. Of these, most were relatively close kin of the head of the household. The largest group, over one-third, were single (and therefore presumably widowed) parents or parents-in-law. A slightly lower number were grandchildren, who, in the majority of cases, did not have their parents resident with them. The remaining significant group was brothers and sisters, making up just under one-sixth. There were only around twenty more distant kin, such as aunts, uncles and 'cousins'. The meaning of these findings can only be inferred. Nevertheless, they strongly suggest that where kin outside the conjugal family were resident in a household, it was usually the result of taking in those who could not care for themselves, including aged parents, orphaned grandchildren, younger brothers and sisters. This, in itself, is instructive about the nature of social obligations towards kin, but it cannot be argued that in early modern England, kin outside the conjugal family were normally resident in households: rather it suggests that they were only resident in exceptional circumstances. In the light of this evidence, the debate over kinship has naturally shifted to investigate the nature of relationships with kin from outside the household.

Most recent historians have either contrasted wider kin unfavourably with the family or with the community at large. In his study of the family life of the seventeenth-century clergyman Ralph Josselin, Macfarlane stressed the relative insignificance of more distant kin. Although a fairly large group of kin was recognised (that is to say mentioned) in Josselin's very extensive and comprehensive diary, only one distant consanguinial relationship (to his father's brother) was found to be of importance. Macfarlane also stressed the greater significance to Josselin of his friends and neighbours [47]. Keith Wrightson and David Levine took up this theme in their study of Terling in Essex. By analysing the proportion of households within the parish that were linked by kinship, they were able to conclude that kinship density within the parish was relatively low, with only 40 to 50 per cent of householders being linked in this way. Furthermore, most of the linked households were related to only one other household, so the network of kinship was also relatively loose [46 *p. 85*]. They argued, therefore, that interaction based on kinship was unlikely. In contrast, interaction with the wider community of neighbours appears to have been vital in everyday life.

It is worth bearing in mind that kinship density is a product of two factors: mobility and the size of the area under examination. One of the most interesting and important facts to emerge about early modern society is the relatively high geographical mobility. This may have been partly the product of the system of service that we have already encountered, which tended to break the links between place or origin and residence at a relatively early age. This meant that employment, and marriage partners, would all have been more likely to be located in another community. This made it difficult for parishes to become agglomerations of descendants of a few families, all inter-related by marriage. It is, however, important to note that English parishes were relatively small, particularly in lowland and urban areas. As a result, even small-scale migrations, to the next village or town, appear to reduce kinship density, but this did not mean that relationships with kin necessarily ended, as small-scale travel was relatively common.

It seems that we should see early modern England not as a series of communities reinforced by the bonds of kinship, but as a much broader web, reaching across communal and geographical boundaries. Although the network of kinship was widely stretched, this does not necessarily make it less significant. The number of kin remained the same for each individual. What were important were the ways in which these kin were regarded and the degree of interaction between them.

One forceful negative response to the emerging consensus on kinship has been to suggest that it had already lost its significance before our period began. Using the detailed manorial court material of Halesowen in Worcestershire, Zvi Razi has argued that before the fifteenth century, a much higher proportion of interactions were with kin [102]. However, the steadily increasing body of work on medieval kinship suggests that it was very similar to that in early modern England. It seems that in most communities, the majority of important interactions were with members of the family, neighbours and only after them with wider kin [32, 103].

However, that is not to say that kin had no role to play. While acknowledging the relative unimportance of more distant kin in most cases, in a seminal article David Cressy, examining the evidence from early modern wills, pointed to the flexibility with which kinship could respond when aid was needed [99]. More forcibly, Miranda Chaytor, working on Ryton in County Durham, has stressed the role of households as focal points for the redistribution of resources among kinship groups [77]. Similarly, Diana O'Hara has emphasised the role of kin in marriage negotiations, even at a relatively humble social level, perhaps indicating that kin as a group could have a stake in the crucial business of forming households [163].

It should also be borne in mind that in early modern England the term 'friend' could be used of both those who were relatives and those who were not [104]. It seems likely then that kinship was one among a number of means by which close and significant relationships could be formed. This raises the issue of which circumstances made kin significant or insignificant. One possibility is that kinship functioned very differently for contrasting social groups. It is also possible that historians have failed to stress sufficiently geographical diversity, which may have had a profound effect on relations with kin where different social and economic systems predominated.

DIVERSITY

In a highly stratified society, with huge contrasts in culture and wealth, it is perhaps rather unsurprising if different social orders are found to exhibit different social attitudes and behaviour. It is clear from their attention to heraldry and genealogy that the nobility and gentry possessed a considerable interest in matters of descent and kinship. But kinship not only provided a proof of status; it also offered a useful resource that could be called upon to further economic or political ambitions. The literate, horse-owning and leisured county elites were the people most likely to be able to maintain and pursue their kinship networks to their best advantage. This was carried out to such a degree that this elite county society has often been seen as an aggregate of kinship networks [37 *pp. 44–8*]. Similarly, while villagers tended to prefer the local gentleman or gentlewoman as godparents to their children, the gentry themselves tended to utilise spiritual kinship as a means of creating and strengthening links within this wider society. It is also notable that the gentry were far more likely to live in households that included kin from outside the conjugal family. This was partly a product of their larger houses, but it also seems to fit in with a pattern of behaviour where wider kinship was of greater significance among this social group.

One good example, highlighted by Rosemary O'Day, is that of the Bagots, a minor gentry family from Blithfield in Staffordshire. Surviving letters from the late sixteenth and early seventeenth centuries, show the head of the family, Walter Bagot, intervening in disputes and problems involving his married siblings; taking his nephew into his house to care for him; negotiating over the marriage of another nephew and godson; and supporting his godsons through their education at Oxford. In O'Day's words, 'the Bagot example shows another dimension of patriarchy in operation, in which the patriarch acted tactfully but decisively to protect the interests of close and distant natural and spiritual kin who were not part of his household' [53 *pp. 68–73*].

Lower down the social scale, among the relatively prosperous yeomen farmers, merchants and professionals of the middling sort, similar, if less pronounced, patterns of behaviour can be seen. It has also been pointed out that, although most houses within an early modern community may not have been connected by kinship, for a significant group of the most stable small farmers, kinship was vitally important [101]. Families from the middling sort, because they had some land to pass on, were more likely to remain in a given area and, since people tended to marry those of similar status, they were also likely to become closely linked to those around them through affinity. In seventeenth-century Myddle, a woodland-pastoral community in Shropshire, there were considerable inter-relationships by kinship among the long-established small farming families [38 *pp. 203–4*]. Among increasingly professionalised clergy and lawyers, there also emerged clerical and legal dynasties, which gave each other mutual support and patronage. Similar networks of support were evident among business families in towns, who were often able to monopolise political power in major regional centres. In these cases, kinship could be extremely useful, and although there was not the same obsession with descent found among the gentry and nobility, where kinship served a purpose, it was often a more significant factor in social relations.

While relatively stable small landholders might have built up local kinship networks and employed them in a similar way to their social superiors, this was a shrinking social category. The evidence indicates that the more mobile, and largely illiterate, rural labouring poor, were less likely to use this resource. However, it has been noted that although this appears to apply to kinship in a rural context, within towns these changes may actually have intensified these forms of relationship. Here populations were more densely packed and mortality generally higher. In these circumstances individuals may have stood a greater chance of being in close proximity to their relatives and may have been forced to rely on them if the vagaries of urban mortality took away members of their closer families.

We will return to the effects of these increasingly common circumstances on family life in the final part of this book, but this observation of differences between town and country also points to the impact of geography and topography on the employment of kinship. It has long been argued that distant kin were more important in some regions of the country than in others. These areas have generally been seen as in the highlands, which predominate in the West and North, where there existed a society largely based on pastoral agriculture [39 *p. 4*, 255 *p. 9*]. Here, as we have already seen, ownership of land was often less important to survival than common rights, such as the ability to graze sheep or cattle on large areas of heath and moor. As a result, it has been argued, the problem of supporting children through inheritance would have been less acute and the imperative to migrate less powerful, resulting in larger collections of kin.

This argument is given some force by the existence of a very different pattern of kinship in the most obvious highland region, on the border with Scotland in the counties of Northumberland, Westmorland and Cumberland. Here existed powerful 'clans' where kinship and obligation were assumed on the basis of surname, such as the Charltons, Robinsons, Dodds and Milburns; the Grahams, Armstrongs and Elliots. These 'wild and misdemeaned people' pursued raids, blackmail and the feud across the border, and among each other, until the seventeenth century [45 *p. 25*, 43 *pp. 60–1*]. However, these 'names' began to lose their collective identity as Tudor and Stuart monarchs stripped their leaders of political influence. In the seventeenth century, individual families began to emerge as the most important units, strongly indicating that this was not a different kinship system, but merely a variation of the same one.

It was once argued that the acute importance of kinship in the borders was also reflected in the rest of the highland regions of England. More recently, where upland and forest communities have been examined in detail, kinship has generally been seen as a relatively unimportant factor. Alan Macfarlane's assessment of kinship in the parish of Kirby Lonsdale in Westmorland, which he describes as an upland parish, led him to conclude that there was no evidence of extensive kinship networks [90 *pp. 75–6*]. However, it is worth noting that surname evidence strongly suggests that mobility was much lower in these areas than in lowland England. Thus, a greater density of kin was present within highland and pastoral communities. In the extensive parish of Almondbury, near Huddersfield in the West Riding of Yorkshire, this reached as high as 75 per cent of households linked by kinship [75 *p. 4*].

What remains debatable is whether these kin played a greater part in the lives of early modern families. Evidence from wills suggests they did not. In fact, the proportion of wills including bequests to wider kin is significantly lower in some highland communities, and tends to be much higher in towns [94, 95]. A variety of explanations can be presented for this evidence, but perhaps the most significant factor is that such parishes, which were less susceptible to the impact of disease, tended to have lower rates of mortality. As a result, close kin may have been more likely to survive and there was less often a need to call on the wider kinship network. Evidently, just because kin were close by, did not mean that they were important in family life.

Although this is an area where much research remains to be done, it seems that one clear characteristic of the English kinship system was its flexibility. It could be adapted to produce something approximating to a clan system, as it continued to do on the Scottish borders into the seventeenth century. It could also be pressed into service where personal or professional necessity dictated, as was so often the case among the nobility, gentry and middling sort. Finally, in an urban context, even the poor appear to have relied upon it as a mechanism for aid and survival. We will return to some of the implications of these variations in the final section of this book. Before that, now that the structures of family life have been outlined, we will turn to the ways in which they fitted together to direct the nature of family life throughout the life cycle.

PART TWO

ANALYSIS – THE PATTERN OF FAMILY LIFE

CHAPTER SIX

INDEPENDENCE AND FAMILY FORMATION

The object of this part of this book is to illuminate the ways in which relationships within families and between kin functioned. As we have already seen, these relations were not fixed, but constantly changing and developing for individuals as they moved through their life course. Accordingly, this section has been divided into four chapters, each focusing not, as is usual, on this individual pattern of change, but on that of the family as a unit, between the beginnings of independence, through its formation in marriage, expansion through the birth of children, to its dissolution by the death of its primary members, the parents.

This was not a clearly defined process, but it is logical to begin with a consideration of the creation of new households through the investigation of the point at which existing households began to fragment. This occurred as the children of a couple began to mature, moving, in the view of many historians, into a new state of youth. As we have seen this often involved a long period of service or apprenticeship, and the nature of this institution is crucial in understanding the ways in which early modern families functioned. Finally, most of those who were to continue family life, emerged from this state to form their own households through the institution of marriage.

THE PROBLEM OF YOUTH

Youth in pre-industrial England has become a popular subject of study in recent years, in part because of the influence of sociological studies of contemporary youth and culture. There is also a recognition that early modern England, with an expanding population and relatively high mortality, was a society with an unusually high proportion of young people. Whether these individuals constituted a 'youth culture' has been much debated. This was sparked off by the sociologist Karl Mannheim, who attempted to differentiate between the existence of generations and youth. The argument follows that, although there were groups of people in the past that we could define as biological adolescents, they lacked a distinct cultural identity [107]. More recently, historians have tended to argue that this distinction is false and that there was such an identity, but its expression was very different from our modern perception of youth. This distinctiveness can be examined in two ways, through the external definitions of youth as a separate stage in the life course and through an investigation of its internal culture and cohesiveness.

In the medieval and early modern periods, it was commonly accepted that the age of seven was a turning point in the life of a child. We have already seen that children could leave home for life cycle service when seven or eight, but eleven to thirteen was probably a more common range. It was from this point, that they began to acquire some of the legal status that marked them off from childhood. Most significantly, females reached the legal age of puberty at twelve and males at fourteen. These were the ages from which individuals could marry, recognising the approximate points from which the different sexes were usually able to be active in sexual reproduction. At this stage, marriage could only take place with parental permission and, as we have already seen, such 'child marriages' were rare, particularly outside the gentry and nobility.

When they were twenty-one individuals had full legal rights over property and this was clearly intended to mark a significant point of transition into adulthood. However, there is evidence that full maturity was not believed to begin until somewhat later. Occasionally, wills mention twenty-five, or even twenty-nine, as the ages of inheritance. As we have already seen, this was also close to the average age of first marriage for men, suggesting this marked the point where they could become full members of society. Thus, law and custom point to gradual and diverse processes by which individuals acquired legal and social status through age. These began, for some, long before modern adolescence, with a move to service or education. They were punctuated by puberty and legal majority, but not complete until marriage, or the death of an individual's parents.

In the context of early modern demography, where the average life expectancy at birth was in the early forties, this was likely to be a significant section of an average life course, roughly a third. However, much of this high mortality was concentrated in the first few years of life, and it is important to bear in mind that for those who survived childhood, this stage formed only a small part of their life experience. It would have been less than one-sixth of the mean life span of those who reached the age of thirty. In the late seventeenth century, those between the ages of fifteen and twenty-four made up less than 17 per cent of the population as a whole [73 *p. 218*]. Nevertheless, it could be argued that this stage saw the formative experiences of individuals' lives, when their ideas, beliefs and economic fortunes were determined.

Even if we accept youth as a social category, what is more difficult is to understand to what degree the individuals within it achieved the hallmark of modern youth, a distinctive youth culture. There are elements that suggest such a pattern. In London, male apprentices shared a common identity within their crafts and gilds, and came together on occasion as a political and military force, most obviously in the civil wars, to lobby for parliament and to fight the king as the major component of the formidable London trained bands [107]. There were also specific occasions in the ritual calendar during which youths predominated. The most obvious was May Day, at the beginning of the agri-cultural year, when potential servants swarmed to market towns to negotiate for employment, but also to dance, play games and drink. Sometimes, these revels went further, with the young electing their own 'lords of misrule', and, as one eyewitness from late sixteenth-century Lincolnshire noted, engaging in 'heathenry, devilry, whoredom, drunkenness, pride and what not' [110 *p. 27*]. But the significance of these circumstances is open to debate. The London trained bands, highly influenced by Puritanism, marked one end of a religious spectrum that would have harshly disapproved of these 'pagan' revels at the other. Moreover, although London was important, with perhaps 20,000 apprentices in the mid-seventeenth century, it was in many ways exceptional, perhaps particularly in terms of service, which across the county as a whole, remained predominantly dispersed and agricultural in nature. It has also been suggested that the revels of youth merely emphasised the subjection to author-ity and labour that the young normally experienced.

An additional problem is that, unlike modern youth, which, since the mid-twentieth century has experienced high levels of disposable income, early modern adolescents were relatively poorly paid and needed their income desperately to secure their future prospects. One area where they may have been able to build their own culture through moderate expenditure was in the buying of cheap print, especially ballads and chapbooks, which were sold for a few pennies. They often specifically addressed themselves to the young [*Doc. 19*]. Many were highly religious in nature and designed, fairly obviously, to constrain youthful behaviour. This may have been, in part, an attempt to justify their existence and does not necessarily mean that they were welcomed by this age group. But they did have a particular emphasis on issues that might appeal to the young, such as courtship [22]. Popular literature may represent the best evidence of a youth culture in this period, but it also demonstrates how that culture fitted into a wider adult world and reflected many of its ideals and concerns.

This evidence does suggest that there was considerable concern over the problems posed by people of this age group, perhaps with renewed emphasis in the seventeenth century, when they were at their largest and most vocal. There was a constant stress on the need for the young to respect their elders, by an extension of the fifth commandment to include not only parents, but also virtually all adults [107]. There was also an emphasis, particularly in more radical religious circles, on catechising; that is the testing of children and servants on a religious catechism of essential beliefs, which was designed to be learnt by rote [111, 123], [*Doc. 9*]. Perhaps these concerns should not be allowed to overshadow other social principles (like those over hierarchy and gender), which were also seen by many as under threat, but it is clear that youth was perceived as posing significant difficulties for the social order.

SERVICE AND APPRENTICESHIP

One set of solutions to the problem of controlling the young was the system of service and apprenticeship. As we have already seen, the English habit of sending the young away from their homes to live and work in other households was frequently noted by visitors to the country. For outsiders, it was often perceived as a sign of indifference to children, but it is likely that the claims that adolescents brought up in another household would be better disciplined, were widely believed in England. It was not a universal practice, being dependent on social standing and economic opportunity. For those lower down in society it was a necessity to find employment for offspring as early as possible, but even parents of the middling sort used it to ensure the training of their children (particularly boys) in a trade, craft or profession. For many, the length of service was long and coincided roughly with the stage between the end of childhood and the beginning of full adulthood. For this reason, it is usually referred to as life cycle service, to separate it from those for whom service was a life-long occupation.

As we have seen, in this period almost one-third of households contained some servants, either domestic or agricultural, and the majority of those in service were adolescents. In some areas these proportions could be very high, with London in the early eighteenth century having as much as 60 per cent of households including servants [122]. Such arrangements often provided relatively short-term employment, for perhaps only a year or two, and could also be interspersed with periods of return to the parental home. Since the probability of householders having servants increased higher up the social scale, and the likelihood of being a servant increased lower down the same scale, it can also be seen as a means of maintaining the social inequalities between rich and poor.

The early modern period was, however, an era of considerable change in the nature of service. In the late middle ages, most servants, whether on the farm, or in the house, were male. However, by the end of the seventeenth century, the majority of domestic servants were 'maids': a term that highlights their unmarried status as well as their gender. Unsurprisingly, the majority of servants in husbandry, who contributed a significant section of agricultural labour, remained male. Therefore, as time went on a distinction developed between the two forms of service emphasised by the gender of those that undertook them [113]. In an age virtually without machines, lacking commercial chemicals, and with relatively limited tools, all work was labour intensive.

Both domestic and farming servants rose early, particularly in the summer, and spent most of their days, except for a reducing number of holidays and to a lesser extent Sundays, engaged in hard or tedious work, be it scrubbing floors, carrying water, or digging ditches and cutting hedges.

Apprenticeship represented a much longer-term, more formal relationship, which implied training in a craft or trade. Throughout our period the overwhelming majority of apprentices were male. There were, however, some skills that were increasingly significant in certain regions of the country, for example lace-making in the East Midlands, which necessitated apprenticeships for women. At the beginning of our period, apprenticeship was often required in order to join a trade organisation or a gild in order to pursue a career and this was only possible after a set period of training. The normal term was seven years, but it was sometimes longer in well-established crafts and shorter in newer ones. However, the position of the medieval gilds had been challenged by the Reformation (which removed their role as lay religious fraternities) and by socio-economic change (which undermined many traditional groups). In addition, the increasing use of compulsory apprenticeship as a solution to the problem of what to do with the children of the poor eroded the social standing of the institution. Finally, the growth of a pool of cheap, unskilled labour and the beginnings of industrialisation also began, as we will discuss in the final part of this book, to make the scheme virtually obsolete in the eighteenth century.

In both service and apprenticeship, the master had the theoretically absolute powers of a father. The thousands of indentures, the legal agreement that initiated apprenticeship, that survive from this period, themselves a fraction of those actually created, almost all take the same form. The master undertakes to supply 'meat, drink, apparel, washing, lodging and all other things', while the servant agrees to 'avoid taverns and alehouses, dice, cards and any other unlawful games . . . fornication [and] matrimony' [18 *p. 8*]. Discipline could be severe and there were a number of instances where masters were prosecuted for killing servants, usually as the result of extreme beatings, but few resulted in convictions [119]. These circumstances seem to suggest that there was considerable violence, and little check upon it. Although, in theory, servants were members of a family, they were rarely treated as such in reality. Revealingly, there was no rite of passage to mark the entry of an individual into the master's family, as is normally the case where adoption or fictive kinship is created, and it seems that this idea of family membership was simply a justification of patriarchal, or occasionally matriarchal, authority.

There may have been more chance for a relationship to build up with apprentices who might also be closer in social standing to their masters. A very few apprentices became affinal kin by marrying their master's daughters and some inherited the estate of a master, but only if he lacked another heir.

More commonly, the relationship was limited to the provision of food, lodging and some payment. Many masters also spent considerable effort on moral and spiritual education, but this again may speak more about concerns over control of the young than incorporation into the family.

As a group, male apprentices were famous for their sexual activity. Sometimes this was with women of their own age and status, but sometimes with prostitutes [112]. Yet, there was little organised prostitution outside London and a few other major urban centres. As we have already seen, there was a relatively low illegitimacy ratio, suggesting that sex between men and women was usually postponed and confined to marriage. It therefore seems likely that contemporary propaganda exaggerated their role in this regard. However, female servants were one of the most common groups bearing illegitimate children, which were frequently, and probably justifiably, attributed to the acts of their masters. In this regard, changes in the nature of domestic service created a large group of potentially exploitable women, many of whom suffered, as a result, both ignominy and poverty.

It seems then that service and the more formal relationship of apprenticeship, often acted as a mechanism for the control, socialisation and education of the young. But it was not simply an isolated social institution, but was linked to those prevailing issues and concerns over gender and hierarchy as well as age. The subordination and oppression of servants and apprentices could be extreme, but in some cases, close relationships could develop between masters and servants. Service thus reflected accurately the mixture of subordination, abuse, co-operation and paternalism that characterised wider early modern society and family life in general.

HOUSEHOLD FORMATION

Although a minority of the population was excluded, youth often ended, and families began, with the formation of a new household through marriage. The process by which this was undertaken is therefore important in understanding family life. The possibility of marriage was, almost throughout society, dependent on the making of a 'good match'. This meant, firstly, that the potential marriage should be valid, by being outside the prohibited degrees of the Church and that both partners should be free from other vows and marriages. It also implied, as the commentator William Perkins put it, 'parity or equality' in age, status and wealth. However, a good match might also necessitate finding a partner who was of slightly greater status or wealth, allowing a degree of social advancement. Obviously, not everyone could achieve this aim and, as a result, the search for partners could resemble a complex economic game. However, the significance of wealth should not be over-stated, other qualities were often highlighted by commentators, including the piety, morality, skills and often the compatibility of potential partners.

Among the nobility and upper-gentry the process was often initiated, or it may be fair to say 'arranged', by parents or guardians. Conduct books usually suggested that the role of parents was to advise and direct, not to dictate. It is also clear from numerous examples that children could get their own way if they were prepared to override their parents' objections. The consent of those entering into a marriage was a crucial principle in law and, it seems, in popular perceptions. It has been argued that this negotiation and calculation indicates a society where sexual and romantic attraction were relatively insignificant. Yet even among the middling sort, at least as early as the sixteenth century, romantic love could be a major factor. Ralph Josselin is just one example of a man who married a woman with whom he had first fallen in love [*Doc. 11*]. As we progress down the social scale, economics and issues of social standing played a lesser part. It therefore seems logical to assume that mutual attraction may have been more significant.

Sons may have had more independence in the choice of partners than daughters, but foreign visitors often noted the considerable freedom given to young English women to travel and visit, which suggests they had greater opportunities for meeting potential marriage partners than their continental counterparts. In these circumstances, it would be logical to expect high levels of sexual promiscuity, but as we have already seen this was not true before industrialisation. One reason may have been that much social interaction between men and women occurred in carefully constructed group activities. For the young the social system was, as John Gillis has observed, 'a homosocial world', where same sex peer groups dominated [159 *p. 22*]. Even the festivals, rituals and games, on St Valentine's Day, May Day and mid-summer, that raised terrible spectres of moral decay in the mind of many a Puritan preacher, were in fact a highly structured and very limited form of social interaction between the sexes. For example, one of the most popular by the seventeenth century, 'Kiss-in-the-Ring', allowed very limited, very public and light-hearted contact between the sexes as they chased and saluted each other. It was thus rare for men and women to experience each other's company in privacy, before they were formally engaged. Women appear to have been particularly dependent on advice and the approval of others, probably because their entire status depended on marrying the right man and in maintaining their reputation for sexual propriety [163]. This may explain why the initiative to begin courtship was usually taken by men.

Courtship could take several years, although periods of around one year appear to have been the most common. Diaries suggest that in practical terms it usually revolved around visits to the woman's parental home, attending rites of passage, trips to nearby towns, visits to alehouses and walks in nearby fields [152, 159]. Most of this activity was conducted in the presence of others, but it is not surprising to find that there is some evidence of this relative freedom leading to pre-marital sexual activity. There was also room for considerable confusion, as under English common law a proposal of marriage, once accepted, was binding. These 'spousals' were often accompanied by the giving of tokens, which were occasionally, but not always, rings. We can see that spousals did allow some young men to obtain sexual favours without an intention to marry, because they occasionally appeared in court for breach of promise. It is also probably true that this system allowed a number of women to acquire the man of their choice as marriage partners, by later claiming such a promise; a vital matter if they had become pregnant.

Usually, before and after formal betrothal, among the propertied classes a lengthy process of careful negotiation was needed that would determine or clarify what each partner would bring into the new household. These discussions often revolved around the potential wife's 'dowry', usually a sum of money from her father's estate. However, it is clear from the evidence of wills, that women also brought other items to a new household, like vital domestic implements such as pots and pans, which would be necessary in its running.

Not all courtship was a careful and well-ordered matter. In a sample of twelve parishes, roughly a quarter of all brides had children within the first eight months of marriage [139, 140]. In some cases, the danger of illegitimate offspring may have forced a match, but in others it may simply indicate that once promises were exchanged, individuals considered themselves married. Despite these problems, the promises were probably genuinely given in most cases, and all the evidence suggests that marriage was considered a very serious and important institution. The suitability of the person with whom that household would be created and shared was a crucial consideration for most people.

The cohesiveness of youth as a social category in early modern England may be open to debate, but it clear that there was a section of the life course which, for the majority, formed an important bridge between childhood and full adulthood. This stage played a vital part in the social and economic order, helping to maintain not only the principle of obedience to elders, but also, in many cases, those distinctions based on gender and status. It also helped to train and socialise future adults, while fulfilling the function of allowing them to gain experience and resources which would be vital in their later lives. Perhaps most significantly, it marked the beginning of both sexual activity and courtship, which were crucial in the formation of the families around which the social system was constructed.

CHAPTER SEVEN

MEN AND WOMEN

The central relationship in early modern family life was that of men and women as husbands and wives. It was the foundation on which the structures of families were built. Its nature, and change in that nature, would therefore have a profound effect on the entire shape of family relationships. However, we have to bear in mind that the importance of conjugal relationships in this period was different from what we might assume today, it was not the norm in social relationships, but the exception. A significant proportion of the population never married. On average this was around 10 per cent, but in some periods the proportion reached as high as one-third [73 p. 260]. Because marriage was relatively late, and mortality high, the average duration of a marriage was also much shorter than now, at about twenty years. As a result, roughly only one-third of the population as a whole would have been married at any given time: today it is more than half. Nevertheless, marriage was a state towards which almost all seem to have aspired and remarriage, after the death of a partner, was very common. Marriage may not have been the statistical norm, but it was the social and psychological norm by which the people of early modern England constructed their society.

THE MARRIAGE RITE

Weddings formed part of the annual social round as well as marking a significant point in the life course. Peak periods in the occurrence of such rites were determined by the ritual and economic year. Many occurred in January and February, after the season of advent had finished, but before the onset of Lent, when the medieval Church had traditionally discouraged marriage and indeed sexual activity, but also before ploughing began. After Easter another pinnacle occurred in April and June, the time when most contracts of service came to an end, leaving former servants free to wed, and a final one occurred after the harvest had been brought in, from October to November.

From the medieval period, marriages should have taken place only in the parish of one of the partners, more often than not that of the bride. This should have been after the Banns, a public proclamation of the intention to marry, were read on three consecutive Sundays. This was designed to give the people who knew the partners best, the opportunity to object to an irregular marriage, vital in an age without bureaucratic central records. The conditions could, nevertheless, be avoided by obtaining a licence from the bishop. In addition, there were relatively large numbers of clandestine marriages, kept secret for a variety of reasons, and which were irregular, but remained legally valid. These reached a peak in the late seventeenth century and were not declared invalid until 1753, when the first systematic reform of marriage law was enforced in what is known as Lord Hardwicke's Act [164].

The act of marriage was more than merely a simple religious ceremony; it was also a collection of complex symbolic traditions. Some of these were very ancient and may have lost their meaning for the participants, but they still embellished the rite in this period, and were all meant to indicate something about the nature of the married state that emerged from it. As a result, weddings, like many rites used by the Church of England, became potential flashpoints for religious differences. We know much about conduct at such occasions because these controversies produced writings both for, and against, popular practice and because of court cases concerned with misconduct at such events.

Wedding traditions varied, not only between different religious movements, but also between social groups and regions of the country. A wedding was an important rite of passage, which marked the end of a process formally begun with betrothal. It was the final point in the transition from individual to couple. It had a large number of participants, including members of the two groups of kin that would be legally joined by the union, and their friends. However, there were also considerable numbers of neighbours present and alms were often given to the local poor to encourage them to attend. This was meant to be not just a family, but also a communal occurrence [159].

The day's ritual events often began with leave-taking by the bride and groom of their same sex peer groups, which was frequently marked by the giving of tokens, such as pairs of gloves, or ribbons. The separation of the bride from her parental home was also, in some parts of the country, clearly marked through ritual. Brides were usually ceremonially dressed, but in their best clothes and not in white until after our period. Occasionally they wore symbols of future domesticity such as knives. The significance of leaving home was often ritually emphasised. The bride might wait with family and friends for 'seekers' or 'guiders' to come from the groom to demand her. This was often met with ritual resistance, such as the shutting of doors or by hiding. When this occurred, it usually cumulated in the groom's friends entering the parental home and hunting for her. However, it was normally the groom, the 'groomsman' (now the bestman) with the rest of his male friends who ended this process by arriving in person to fetch her [78 *pp. 339–40*]. One tradition was that on leaving the bride was not supposed to look back at her former home, symbolising her separation from the family of orientation.

All parties then processed to the church for the ceremony, sometimes over a considerable distance. This was not always straightforward as the path of the bride and groom was often barred by neighbours, they could also be locked in a house, prevented from entering or leaving the church or churchyard until a toll was paid, traditions known variously as the 'chaining', 'footing', 'cock-walking', 'pitchering', 'petting', or 'pennying' [154 *p. 85*]. This was perhaps to defuse ritually any disagreements about the wedding taking place, but also a useful source of cash for some of the participants.

Within the entire ritual process, the ceremony at the church may have been less important than in more recent times. The medieval Church had been reluctant to make it central and Puritans came to prefer a civil ceremony. Before Lord Hardwicke's Act, it was not clear that a church service was essential for a marriage to be valid. Vows of chastity had already been exchanged at betrothal and were merely being confirmed here. The blessing of the ring and the confirmation of the bride's dowry (symbolised by placing coins on the priest's book) were probably seen as the more important elements and a reminder of the economic considerations behind the marriage ceremony. At the end of the rite it was often the parson and not the groom, who was expected to kiss the bride. There might then be the sharing of cake or cheese and biscuits within the church to symbolise the unity created by the marriage. Finally, garters might be seized as tokens from both bride and groom by young men.

Outside the church, the couple was often greeted by 'rough music' on pots and pans, as well as peeling bells. Then a celebratory meal, the bride-ale, was normally provided. This was sometimes paid for by the bride's father, but perhaps more often by the couple. If they were poor there might be a 'penny-wedding', where all the guests contributed a small sum to the festivities. The meal was often at the bride's former home, but lower down the social scale the local ale-house seems to have been a popular venue. A cake, or small cakes, made of flour, salt and water would be eaten and wine would be symbolically shared, sometimes in the same 'knitting-' or 'bride-cup'. Finally, the party moved on to the couple's new home where they might witness the newly weds enter their bed or even help them undress and where they would, finally, be left alone to begin their new life [159 *pp. 74–5*].

Most of these practices were disliked and discouraged by Puritans, and were dying out from the seventeenth century. This process of de-ritualisation was almost certainly completed first, and most thoroughly, in the South of England, where Puritanism was most successful. During the Interregnum, between 1649 and 1660, when, albeit briefly, Puritanism became the state creed, church marriage was abolished altogether and weddings were carried out before Justices of the Peace, but this process was reversed with the Restoration of the monarchy. Nevertheless this movement came, in time, to remove many of these 'superfluous' practices associated with the rite, and may have undermined something of its communal nature, making it much more a matter for family and friends.

SEX

Baptismal registers indicate that most sexual activity took place in the period between late spring and early summer. The season of least sexual activity was the late summer and autumn, which, in the sixteenth century, was followed by a small peak in the period around late December and early January. These circumstances can be partly explained by the pattern we have already seen of marriages across the year and by the necessities of the agricultural year. These factors suggest that sexual activity was common immediately after marriage, but least likely when the demands of work were greatest. It also indicates that conceptions were being avoided when pregnancy might interfere with the demands of work and that, at the beginning of our period, the celebrations associated with festivals, particularly that of advent, presented opportunities and circumstances in which sexual activity was more probable [73 *pp. 291–2*].

Attitudes to sex were superficially very clear and almost universally agreed in this period. The only form of sex that was considered correct by most commentators, was that within marriage, for the procreation of children and in the missionary position. However, there were significant differences between the emphasis on the value of sexual activity within marriage. Many Catholic commentators tended to see all sex as an evil, if a necessary one. In contrast, Protestants, perhaps particularly the more radical Puritans in England, following the lead of many thinkers of the Renaissance, had a more positive view of sex within marriage. They tended to depict it as something actively good: a confirmation of the validity of the union as well as a necessary safety valve for containing sexual passions.

Ideas on sex derived, ultimately, from ideas about differences between the sexes. It has been argued that there were two views of women. One saw them as sexually neutral, and inert; the other saw them as more passionate (and dangerous) than men. The balance of these two views has been much debated. It has been argued that because of increasing dominance of the latter view towards the middle of our period, it became the orthodoxy that sex was not to be over-indulged in. The early modern opinion was of the need for 'matrimonial chastity', that is to say moderation within marriage. The idea was that men should satisfy their wives, but not excite so much libido as would enflame their passions.

Medical opinion, based on Aristotelian ideas of the balance of humours within the body, argued that excess was medically dangerous, at least for men. The diarist John Evelyn thought that 'too much frequency of embraces dulls the sight, decays the memory, induces gout, palsies, enervates and renders effeminate the whole body, and shortens life' [*55 p. 497*]. Some argued against total abstinence as well, however; abstinence was expected of the majority of the population who were not married. How far down the social scale these ideas permeated is extremely difficult to judge and we will return to this problem in the final part of this book. One might suspect that most people were largely unaware of them.

The common people had their own codes of sexual behaviour and often their own means of dealing with breaches of them. For example, cuckolds (men whose wives had had illicit sex) might wake to find horns placed outside their houses (because it was believed cuckolds grew invisible horns). Verses and songs were also circulated, sometimes in written form, as a means of condemning and accusing members of the community of unpopular practices [138] [*Doc. 14*]. There were also rituals known variously as the 'charivari', 'ridings', 'rough music', or 'skimmingtons'. These were devices by which members of a community highlighted (and therefore punished) perceived unacceptable behaviour through a public ritual. The victim, or a substitute, was usually led around the village, either on a horse, or pole, and pelted with stones or mud, often with the supposed offence acted out in the process. The most common perceived offenders punished in this way were henpecked husbands, but the battering of wives was also disliked [143]. It seems that the popular perception of married life was one where sexual impropriety was not allowed, and in which, although clearly the man must be the head of his own household, he did not have the right to overuse his authority [Plate 3].

Interesting as these events appear, the most significant actions may have been the ability of the local elite to report offenders to the church courts and the informal power of gossip. Gossip was a highly significant sanction, but it is difficult to investigate because it is usually so trivial that it does not often surface in the historical record. Contemporaries certainly believed it was an activity largely undertaken by women. It was also probably an extremely frequent occurrence. In one case investigated in detail by Steve Hindle, in 1625 Margaret Knowsely, the servant of a Cheshire clergyman, accused him of rape in at least some forty conversations, almost all of them with women [131]. In this way, women can be seen as having an essential role in defining the moral bounds of the community and the standing of its inhabitants. This was a factor evidenced by the growing recourse to the courts to bring civil actions for slander when individuals felt their reputation was in danger [129, 130, 147]. However, as these circumstances indicate, gossip could also be malicious and must have destroyed the reputations of many innocent people as well as keeping in check the actions of the majority.

Moreover, these sanctions were not applied equally to both sexes. This 'double standard', by which men had greater licence for illicit sexual activity, is, however, a complex issue. It is most evident in the upper reaches of society where famous cases of mistresses and infidelity abound. Local notables were also insulated to a degree by their social standing from the effects of popular condemnation and perhaps also from prosecution. Lower down in society, a woman's reputation, arguably the most important single factor in securing her future through marriage, has often been seen as clearly more significant than that of a man, whose reputation was usually more concerned with financial honesty and a willingness and ability to honour debts [148]. As a result, even though women may have had a certain social prominence and control through gossip, they were also more likely to be its victims.

However, the idea that men were isolated from the problems of sexual reputation has been convincingly challenged by Bernard Capp [136]. Many men, perhaps particularly those of some significant social status, did have their reputation damaged by accusations and suspicions of misconduct. The fact that more women than men were prosecuted for sexual offences may have more to do with the fact that their actions were likely to be made evident through pregnancy, rather than marking a lack of concern with pursuing offending men. It is also true that, before the eighteenth century, moralists and commentators universally condemned the double standard and that once a couple were married they shared a joint responsibility for defending their moral reputation.

Despite these sanctions, some individuals stood outside these moral boundaries. Many illegitimate pregnancies may have been the sad product of serious but failed courtships; however, there were others who stand out in the records as persistent offenders against the morals of community and society. In terms of illegitimacy not all historians are convinced that there was, as Laslett termed it, 'a bastardy-prone sub-culture', but there were certainly 'repeaters', women who are identifiable for numerous illegitimate births, often to different men. Within a community these women were often connected to each other by family ties and usually came from the poorer social orders. They serve as an important reminder that some did not accept the almost universal public morals of the majority, but the reasons for their actions are difficult to discern. It is possible to argue that they represented a different set of moral values, a sector of society without morals, an indication that sexual pleasure was significant for some, or that prostitution was more widespread than might be otherwise assumed.

There has also been considerable interest in recent years in other forms of sexual activity, including, most obviously homosexuality. Sexual relations between women were almost unmentioned in the records and those between men were always treated with total hostility and repugnance and references to the fate of the biblical cities of Sodom and Gomorrah. Sodomy was a capital offence from 1563. Nevertheless, there is some evidence of a sub-culture of homosexual relations, particularly in elite and court circles. The evidence always needs to be treated with extreme caution, as moral depravity, like heresy, was a useful charge to put on one's enemies and unlikely to be confirmed by those involved [142]. However, by the eighteenth century, at least in London, there appears to have emerged a wider movement, based on clubs and café culture [150]. Despite this, homosexuality remained a subject of horror in the eyes of most, although it was rarely prosecuted outside the occasionally *cause célèbre*.

MARRIED LIFE

The theory of patriarchal authority underlay all family relationships in this period. In 1590, William Perkins defined a husband as 'he that hath authority over the wife'. In 1622, William Gouge drew a common analogy, describing him as 'king in his owne house' [23 *pp. 90–1*]. Married women could not normally hold property and could not represent themselves in law. A husband was also free to administer limited corporal punishment to a wife. In most circumstances, a woman was seen as having no right to disobey her husband's will. Tyrannical husbands, like kings, had merely to be endured. The virtues of womanhood were submissiveness and silence; the vices were disobedience and a 'prattling' tongue [*Docs 15 and 16*]. Commentators, who were, of course, for the most part male, generally accepted that women were physically, mentally and emotionally inferior to men. They were the 'weaker vessel', that a husband had to discipline, direct and protect.

Needless to say, this image, widespread as it might be in the literature of the period, rarely matched up to reality. The fact that so many women were punished for the crime of scolding (using sharp language) indicates not only concerns about female disobedience, but also the failure to prevent it [*Doc. 13*]. There are also a number of instances where women took on part of their husband's charge, most obviously in figures from the nobility and gentry. One such was Lady Margaret Hoby of Hackness in the East Riding of Yorkshire, who, towards the end of the sixteenth century, frequently had to take on the duties of running the household and estate while her husband was away in parliament or pursuing Catholics [10]. Lower down the social scale, women could enjoy their own social life. Married women presided at events such as birth, or rituals such as churching [177]. We have also already seen the major contribution they made to community life through work and gossip.

The picture of the monarchical husband must also be contrasted with a stress on partnership in the same conduct books. There was considerable emphasis on co-operation and friendship between husband and wife. Where records are sufficiently complete, they suggest that most men tended to consult their wives on important matters, such as large purchases, or the careers and marriages of children. There was also a stress in these same conduct books on romantic love. William Gouge likened love to glue that bound the couple together, while William Whately defined this emotion within marriage as a love that exceeds all others. To modern eyes, this may seem at odds with the known practice of 'arranged' marriages that were most prevalent among the higher social orders (the very groups most likely to read this advice) and even with the economic negotiations that dominated matches lower down the social scale. However, it is important to stress the expectation that love would flourish and grow after marriage, which can be contrasted with the modern view that marriage is the potential outcome of love.

What is more difficult to discern is how much all this was carried out in practice. Model letter books devoted a considerable amount of space to the subject of love and Macfarlane's study of letters from the period indicates that it was a widespread concept [162]. A number of diaries also indicate that husbands were often very affected by the deaths of spouses. In the seventeenth century, women's diaries also indicate deep affection for, and even intense relationships with, their husbands. All these sources are from the higher ranks of society. Lower down we are forced to rely on studies of matrimonial court cases, which, like those undertaken by Martin Ingram and Ralph Houlbrooke, also seem to indicate that these ideas were commonplace and that romantic love (developing within marriage) was a universal ideal [144, 227] [Plate 2].

However, not all marriages were happy working partnerships, and then, as now, disharmony and breakdown could occur. When this happened, the relationship could become, as William Whately put it, 'a little hell'. The notebooks of Richard Napier, who acted as the equivalent of a psychologist in early seventeenth-century London, reveal that poor marital relationships could be a considerable source of anxiety to women. Diaries, which were most often written by men, can also show worries about the breakdown of married relationships. Lawrence Stone estimated that between 1570 and 1659 one in ten of the marriages of peers broke down into disunity. Occasionally this was due to infidelity, but more normally due to growing arguments [170].

This was particularly problematic because there was almost no divorce in early modern England. Some troubled marriages did receive annulments (which technically meant the marriage had not taken place), usually on grounds of pre-contract, but these were very rare. Officially, there were no annulments for adultery, until a small number of cases were carried through under a new act of parliament from the late seventeenth century. However, this almost only applied to the very wealthy and was an option almost exclusively confined to men. Lower down the social scale the church courts could, in dire circumstances, offer separation 'from bed and board' on grounds of adultery or cruelty [144 *pp. 146–7*]. When these arrangements became longer term, alimony (usually of one-third of an estate) was awarded to wives to help them to survive. However, most separations were permitted in the hope of a later reconciliation and neither party would have been able to remarry legally. These options only existed in a tiny majority of cases and it seems an unavoidable conclusion that many may have lived, as the diarist Henry Newcome noted of one couple, in 'secret unkindness' [12 *p. 85*].

At the bottom of the social scale, those men who had little stake in land or their local reputation did at least have the option of deserting their partners. The records of poor relief are filled with cases of abandoned wives and children. Some of these men may have simply travelled for economic reasons and gradually decided not to return, or have died while away. Others may well have gone to avoid a unwelcome marriage or other commitments. It was fear of these circumstances and their moral and economic consequences that lay behind the passing of an act against bigamy in 1603. However, these remained rare circumstances. For most men and almost all women, it was the high mortality rate that ended partnerships. For some this must have seemed like a blessed release, but the evidence strongly suggests that for most it was an occasion for grief.

Even when affection was lacking, most partners appear to have achieved a form of equilibrium that allowed them to conduct their everyday lives without a breakdown into acrimony or violence. It is important to point out that late marriage and high mortality meant that the relationship was a more temporary arrangement. It is also likely that the majority accepted the model of care and obedience that characterised public thinking on marriage and that this helped to make it a success in most cases.

In early modern England, marriage marked the creation of a new family much more clearly than it does today. Weddings were, for that reason, much more public and communal events. It is also evident that the activities of married couples were often impinged upon by the attitudes and beliefs of those outside the household. Therefore, the roles of married couples were often defined by common opinion in the local community. In part, this was because marriage was also the means by which sexual activity was regulated. Additionally, it is clear that married relationships were structured within the framework of romantic love that was accepted by almost every social group. Occasionally, the relationship broke down, but largely it provided companionship and emotional and financial security for both partners.

CHAPTER EIGHT

PARENTS AND CHILDREN

As we have already seen, until the 1980s the central debate over childhood in the early modern period was between those who believed that parental relationships were cold and those who argued they were similar to modern emotional ties. It is now impossible to support the former argument, but it remains necessary to advance the debate over childhood in order to understand the nature of past relationships between adults and children in detail and in their own terms. This chapter will examine these relationships through an investigation of the attitudes towards childbirth, infants, and older children.

HAVING CHILDREN

The obvious answer to the central question of why people in early modern England had children is that, lacking contraception, they had little or no choice. This is not entirely true, as there were some options available, including abstention, *coitus interruptus*, and breast-feeding. Of these breast-feeding, or lactation, was probably the most significant, as it inhibits conception (although not with absolute certainty) and, as we will see, was often practised for some time after birth. There is also evidence of a limited knowledge of physiology that may have helped. However, this was largely based on the inaccurate ideas of Aristotle, and merged into herbal medicine and folklore, which made it highly unreliable [175] [*Doc. 18*]. Barrier methods of contraception, using fish or animal skins, were available from at least the mid-seventeenth century and possibly to a much wider social range than has been assumed in the past. However, their primary function may have been to limit the risk associated with sexually transmitted diseases, rather than the prevention of conception.

Despite these methods, once married, couples rarely enjoyed a long period of income without expenditure on children; perhaps four-fifths of couples who would have children did so within two years [139 *p. 60*]. If individuals in the past did have a degree of choice, why did they exercise it towards having children? The reasons are in many ways similar to today. There was an accepted duty to populate the world and carry on the family line, particularly in the higher social ranks, but these desires had echoes throughout society. It was also part of the social role and expectations of married couples, with childlessness being generally regarded as a sad plight, although infertility was not grounds for legal separation. Motherhood, in particular, was seen as the defining characteristic of women and gave them a unique value in society. From the medieval period, children were seen as a gift from God. At the lower end of the social scale, although initially very expensive, offspring were a potential economic prop and, for all social groups, they could provide care in old age or infirmity. Finally, it is possible that one major reason for having children was the obvious one, that many married couples liked them.

At least among the higher social orders, married pregnant women, then as now, appear to have derived some temporary status, and attention, from their physical state and were often the subject of considerable pride among their husbands. Logic suggests that this was less marked lower down the social scale, where women would often have to continue to undertake physical work very late into the pregnancy. Attitudes to pregnancy outside marriage were, of course, very different, and part of the mechanism that was so successful in keeping most sexual activity within matrimony was the extreme moral and social stigma associated with illegitimacy. Unmarried mothers were singled out by their pregnancy as fornicators and their children were marked for life as being of dubious status. In these circumstances, many women tried to hide their pregnancies for as long as possible. Some attempted difficult, and frankly dangerous, processes of abortion, while others committed infanticide.

In the state courts, prosecutions and convictions for this last offence increased significantly after 1624, when a new statute was passed. Some of these cases may have been what we now define as 'cot death' or 'sudden infant death syndrome', but this is most common between the ages of two and four months and the evidence suggests that most of these instances were outside this age band. Large numbers were new-born children. The 1624 act made concealment of a still-born child, an obvious defence against the charge, also a capital offence, and this partly explains the rise in prosecutions [20 *pp. 61–2*]. However, the overall infanticide rate was certainly not high enough to indicate widespread abuse of children as some authors once suggested. It is also true that an increase in prosecutions for this action can also be taken to indicate intolerance of the crime, which suggests the development of a more caring society.

Most infanticides appear to have been the product of desperation. It is worthwhile considering the all too frequent circumstances of a serving girl who found herself pregnant. If she could not marry the father, which was often the case, she faced not only loss of employment, but also of reputation on which her future marriage prospects depended. Moreover, she was likely to be ostracised by the community and even by her family, while she was left with an extra mouth to feed. Perhaps most interestingly, as with infant mortality in general, there was no significant distinction between boys and girls as victims of this crime. All the evidence suggests that male children would have been more welcome than females and if this was a society where infants were routinely abused and murdered, girls should have been more likely to die than boys.

The inference seems to be that children were generally accepted, even welcomed. This view receives some support from biographical sources. In her survey of early modern diarists, Linda Pollock could not find any indication that children were unwanted. Many authors were simply silent on the matter, while some expressed genuine pleasure, commonly seeing children as a blessing from God. The only serious reservations were where the number of children were such that economic resources might be stretched until they were too thin [195 *pp. 204–5*].

In the early modern period, childbirth was actually not very much more dangerous to the mother than it is now. Between sixteen and twenty-five women in every thousand died in childbirth. Now the figure is lower, but not dramatically so, at around twelve in a thousand [180]. Of course, most people in the period did not appreciate this and pregnancy, but particularly childbirth, were seen as times of great danger [Plate 1]. Without any anaesthetic and with the risk of a difficult birth, it would also have been very painful for the mother and harrowing for potential fathers. These concerns were reflected in the relief and thanksgiving that tended to follow a successful delivery, which can be seen in both the nature of public ceremonies and expressions in private records.

Women were, of course, in an age without any real understanding of the mind and without medicines to treat imbalances in body chemistry, far more subject to the effects of post-natal depression than is the case today. These circumstances are probably hidden in the deaths of mothers soon after childbirth which are sometimes recorded in parish registers. These were occasionally actually listed as suicides, as in the case of Agnes Littlewood from Almondbury in the West Riding of Yorkshire who in 1575 took herself from her childbed and threw herself down a well, as the vicar recorded, 'by the instigation of the devil' [17 *p. 94*].

Birth was very much more dangerous for the child, with perhaps one in three of all pregnancies ending in a miscarriage or a still birth [179]. These circumstances were probably improved by the presence of midwives, who tended to supervise the largely female event of childbirth. Most midwives were, however, untrained and often of marginal status in the community. The seventeenth century saw the arrival of the *man-wives* (male midwives), who often criticised the ignorance of poor peasant women, but who themselves may have been as much of a danger as benefit to many women in labour. The most famous man-wives were members of the Chamberlain family of London, responsible for introducing the use of forceps into birth. However, such services were available mainly to the wealthy and those in the capital [183].

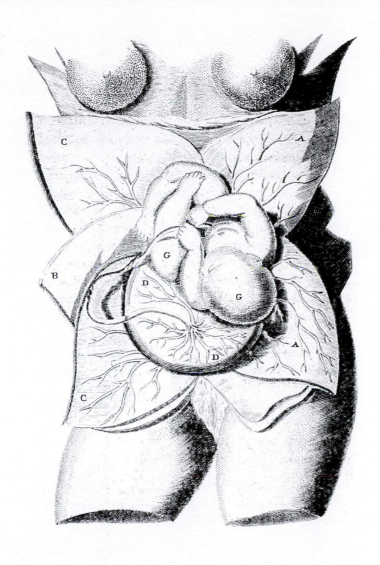

Position of a Child in the Womb just before Delivery

1. The state of medical knowledge about childbirth.

Mary Evans Picture Library.

2. Companionate marriage in the eighteenth century.

Mary Evans Picture Library.

3. The image of a battered husband.
Mary Evans Picture Library.

4. A godly household in the sixteenth century.

Mary Evans Picture Library.

5. A godly household in the eighteenth century.
Mary Evans Picture Library.

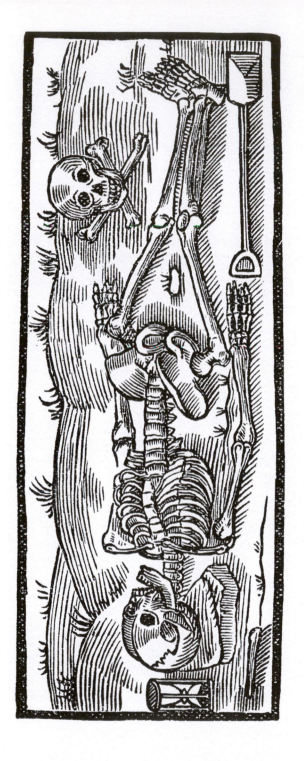

A foggy dimness doth his sight assail,
Striking into his head; his eyes they fail;
His tongue does faulter, and his hands they shake,
And with the Palsie every limb does quake.

6. The depiction of the dead.
Mary Evans Picture Library.

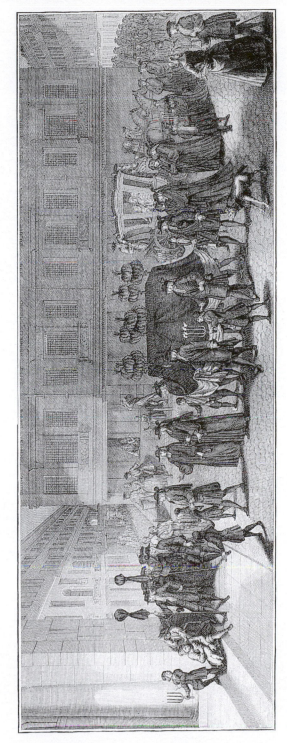

7. The funeral of a wealthy individual.
Mary Evans Picture Library.

8. The impact of enclosures on a rural family.
Mary Evans Picture Library.

Most births progressed without the need for any assistance and it was believed that the poor gave birth much more easily than the rich, suggesting that little interference was really necessary. They were also expected to recover much more quickly than the wives of the nobility and gentry did. It is therefore debatable whether most mothers could undertake the ritual and social isolation usually proscribed for the first month after birth. This should have ended with the ceremony of churching, which marked the return of a woman to church and community. This has been seen variously as a thanksgiving for deliverance from the pain and risks of childbirth and a popular rite of purification from its pollution. It survived the Reformation, but was objected to strongly by Puritans, although it was still being carried out in the 1950s in some parts of the country. Recent thinking has tended to downplay the ritual elements and emphasise the social occasion where women enjoyed a certain prominence, basking in their uniqueness as mothers [176, 177].

INFANTS

In the medieval period, the assumption was that only the baptised could be saved and most commentators suggested that at death unbaptised children went to a state of limbo, but there is some evidence that many feared they would be consigned to Hell. As a result, babies were baptised very rapidly, usually within three days. Therefore, in this period, the seasonality of baptisms naturally closely followed those of conceptions and of births. They tended to peak in the period between February and April, falling towards July and hitting a lesser peak in the autumn [73 *p. 228*]. This was frequently a private ceremony, often in an otherwise empty church, and lacking the parents (who were not allowed to attend). If there were a danger that the child might die, the ceremony would often be undertaken immediately by the midwife. These practices were discouraged after the Reformation. Baptism ceased to be considered necessary for salvation by the Church of England and reformers also wanted it to become a public event. In this, they were largely successful, tending to make it part of Sunday service. As a result, the interval between birth and baptism gradually widened. By 1655–56 three-quarters of children were not baptised until after two weeks in one London parish [174 *pp. 462–3*]. There is some evidence that this was part of a process of change in ideas about the nature of new-born children. The concept of original sin had meant that infants were seen as born into corruption and even demonic possession and pure only after baptism. However, by the late sixteenth century, it seems to have been increasingly common for children to be seen as born pure, but corrupted by the world [210 *pp. 266–87*].

In the same period, the role of godparents was probably declining. In medieval Catholicism, they had theoretical responsibilities to care for children if their parents failed to do so. These were downplayed in the Reformation and Puritans wanted to abolish the institution altogether, because it lacked a scriptural basis and distracted from the role of natural parents in educating their children. However, there is evidence that it remained vital into the mid-seventeenth century, when it was temporarily abolished during the Interregnum. When it was restored with the monarchy in 1660, it seems to have been on a more limited basis. Records of godparents in baptismal registers are very rare from this point and gifts to godchildren less frequent in wills. Godparents also began to lose one of their major functions in the ceremony of baptism, where they, rather than the parents, had given children their first names, usually their own [181]. The institution was further undermined by the rise of religious sects, most obviously the Baptists, who practised adult, rather than infant, baptism.

Even in the late medieval period, it is clear that the primary responsibility for the care and upbringing of children lay with the natural parents. That is not to say that they always undertook this process in ways that we would now necessarily recognise. One area that has received considerable criticism is the practice of swaddling. This involved either the tying of a cloth, or the wrapping of swaddling bands in mummy fashion, around a child, rendering it unable to move. However, swaddling was probably only employed for the first two or three months when the movement of babies is very limited and therefore was not simply an uncaring mechanism of child control. It may have been unhygienic, but this was not a concept parents in this period understood. Instead, many probably felt they were benefiting their child by helping its bones to grow straight and by preventing them from scratching themselves [33 *p. 132*].

According to Linda Pollock, Philippe Ariès characterised the attitude to children before the sixteenth century as one where they were ignored, although, in fact, Ariès was careful to state that he did not believe that children 'were neglected, forsaken or despised' [184 *p. 125*]. She is probably correct to suggest that the crying of infants was not simply disregarded and modern studies indicate that it is, as every parent will be aware, very hard to ignore [195 *p. 224*]. However, if it is disregarded, a child will suppress the perfectly natural crying reflex. The degree to which this was done varied then, as now, from family to family. One reason why diaries do not appear to contain many references to the crying of infants may be that it had a limited effect on diarists, who were predominately male and wealthy. They were therefore somewhat insulated from it, either literally, by distance and thick walls, or because of the likely division of labour in the household. It is important to remember that this was a society where service was a common feature and in wealthier households female servants would often have carried much of the burden of care. Lower down the social scale, and on the female side of the gender divide, it would have been impossible to ignore the cries that punctuate the normal development of children.

Despite discouragement from the Church, and almost all commentators, the use of wet nurses to care for and breast-feed infants remained a frequent practice among members of the gentry and urban elites. This was, and continues to be, seen as limiting the parent/child bonding process in these formative stages and has been taken by some historians to suggest that there was a general indifference to children before the eighteenth century. It also appears to have considerably reduced the likelihood of the child's survival as mortality rates among nursed children were much higher than among the general population. Despite this image, it is clear from diaries and letters that many of the literate classes took immense pains in selecting nurses and it was a matter of considerable anxiety. Here it is appropriate to cite the acute observation of Ralph Houlbrooke, that 'the biggest contrast in the quality of care and consequent effects on the infant's prospects lay not between maternal and wet-nursing but between good and bad wet-nursing' [33 *p. 133*]. It is also important to note that it only applied to a small minority of all families: most women from the lower social orders, in rural areas and less established towns (where no systems of nursing had yet developed), had no choice but to suckle their own children. Evidence of diaries indicates that this was often a painful, difficult, but also emotionally satisfying process.

The age at which children were weaned varied considerably, even within the same family. Six of the children of John Dee, the sixteenth-century astrologer and diarist, were breastfed until between seven-and-a-half and sixteen-and-a-half months old [195 *p. 220*]. The mean age appears to have been between these extremes, at just over one year old. However, this age appears to have fallen in the eighteenth century, to less than ten months. This was perhaps partly due to the greater availability of food substitutes and feeding vessels, but also a product of the abandonment of the practice of wet-nursing. Women suckling their own children were likely to terminate it earlier than those earning their living from the practice [187 *pp. 223–40*]. The evidence of diaries indicates that this period was a difficult one for children and adults alike. Similarly, teething, which occurs at vastly different ages and with various levels of disruption, was also a time of particular anxiety and distress.

In contrast, the transition to independent walking and the uttering of a child's first words, provided almost universally welcome milestones in child development. Then, as now, the ages at which these events occurred varied greatly, at anything between nine and sixteen months in eighteenth-century diaries, for the first independent steps, and sixteen months to two years for the first words. Both these figures suggest that child development was not notably deficient compared with today. Children were encouraged to walk by holding hands and by reins attached to clothes. They were also encouraged to speak and, at least by the end of our period the repetition to them of words like 'da-da' and 'pa-pa' are clearly evident in diaries [195 *pp. 225–30*].

Once they were able to walk, young boys probably spent roughly the same amount of time with both parents, while girls appear to have been disproportionately in the company of their mothers [32 *p. 184*]. Medieval commentators tended to imply that young children should be allowed to learn through shared activities, at their own pace [200]. Most of their time was probably spent in play. However, we are woefully ignorant of the activities they undertook. This is in part because the everyday lives of children were so rarely recorded. Although Ariès attempted a pioneering investigation of this aspect of childhood, his sources meant it was largely confined to the French court. References to play in diaries tend to express dislike of the activity because it distracted from education [195 *p. 237*]. These entries do indicate that girls had dolls and more structured play for boys tended to revolve around bat and ball games, including 'trap-ball' and 'wicket'. We can surmise that certain games, like 'Here we go round the mulbury bush' were played, because the rhymes associated with them are of some antiquity. Of the 'traditional' rhymes collected by Iona and Peter Opie, over 80 per cent probably originated from before the end of the eighteenth century: perhaps almost a quarter from the sixteenth century or before [11 *p. 7*]. However, many were adult in origin, few were connected to actual games and we have little idea of how knowledge of these rhymes was spread across the country. We are even more ignorant about everyday informal play, except on those odd occasions where it resulted in a tragedy, such as children who fell into water while staring at their reflections [32 *pp. 185–6*].

OLDER CHILDREN

Around the age of seven, boys began to dress in coats and breeches. Play would begin to give way to work, training and, if available, formal education. As we have already seen, lower down the social scale the need for children to make an economic contribution to the household may have become greater. They would rapidly, and necessarily, be given tasks to learn and perform that were of economic value. These included herding and shepherding of livestock, or carrying out a simple part of a manufacturing process. They would also begin to learn vital skills from their parents, such as needlework for girls.

Education outside the family took many forms in early modern England. It might involve private tuition, enrolment in a petty or parish school, and eventually, for the better-off boys, a move to a grammar school. Much of this spectrum of educational institutions was highly unstable, often dependent on individual initiatives, with tutors, master and institutions coming and going with incredible speed. By the end of our period, perhaps half the parishes in the country had some form of schooling at any given time. These were not, however, evenly distributed or evenly utilised by all social ranks. The cost of around a half-penny a day was too much for many labouring families, and the need to have children work, particularly in times of intense agricultural activity such as harvest, meant that what education they received was likely to be fragmented [190]. Nevertheless, the trend to endow 'free' schools, which was particularly intense in the late Tudor and early Stuart periods, has been seen as ushering in an 'educational revolution' [201]. Sometimes these were established by a single benefactor, sometimes by remarkable community effort, as at Willingham in Cambridgeshire where 102 villagers subscribed to found a school in 1593 [44 *p. 193*]. However, although often intended for the children of the community as a whole, and occasionally for the poor in particular, those schools that survived often did so by catering for the social elite.

Nevertheless, our best measure of literacy, signatures, suggests that this activity did have profound effects on the basic education of the population as a whole. This was most marked among men, of whom perhaps two-thirds could read and write by the end of the eighteenth century. To a lesser degree (and at a later date) there was a similar effect among women, of whom perhaps two-fifths could read and write by the end of our period. Literacy was also socially biased towards the top ranks of society, which were almost universally literate by the end of this era, but it was skewed in other ways, for example towards urban populations, with their concentration of craftsmen and local notables, who were far more likely to embrace literacy. However, these figures mean that by the end of the eighteenth century, only two countries in Europe (Scotland and Sweden) had higher literacy rates than England [19 *pp. 61–3*].

The widespread shift towards a literate society was not confined to the classroom; it was only possible because it went hand in hand with the massive increase in popular print, which played a great part in providing an incentive for even the very poor to read. However, much of this transformation was achieved in crowded single rooms, often in houses or in shops, where children of all ages were instructed together. Slates were used to teach writing by copious copying. Boys might then go on to undertake basic number work, while lower expectations for girls were often marked by a move to needlework. This education also included religious instruction and the instilling of obedience and manners. The hours of attendance tended to increase as educational institutions became more formal and it is likely that discipline did also.

Concern with the discipline of children was considerable. Affection was mixed with fears of spoiling a child. In the early part of our period, all religious groups were pessimistic about the nature of children, because of the doctrine of original sin, which depicted children as naturally inclined to evil. This probably led to some corporal punishment. Lawrence Stone detected a shift from a parental relationship based on the 'stick' of beatings to one based on the 'carrot' of affection and the threat of its withdrawal, but the evidence remains highly inconclusive. Many of the contrasts he points to do not mark differences between different eras, but between parents and other figures of authority. It is hardly surprising to find that parents were less likely to use such physical forms of discipline than teachers and masters [55 *p. 435*]. The same natural reaction also implies that orphans or those separated from their parents were far more likely to experience physical punishment and even abuse. Yet in general, this is not symptomatic of an uncaring society, but one where parental love played a crucial part in limiting physical punishment. Awareness of this problem was probably one motive behind the sending of older children away to work, to be trained or educated in another household, as parents felt that others could correct their children better than they could themselves.

In early modern England, as now, having children was for many the *raison d'être* of existence, it was also often difficult to avoid. Children's lives could be, and frequently were, very short, but for many, they were still seen as a blessing from God. There is evidence that the functions of parenthood we associate with the role may have been becoming more concentrated in the natural parents and attitudes towards the nature of children and childhood may also have been changing. However, amid all of this, many of the ideas that we now take for granted about children and childhood also applied in the past.

CHAPTER NINE

BROKEN FAMILIES

Just as families in early modern England were formed with the creation of new households, usually around the institution of marriage, so they were also dissolved as essential members of the household died. However, the early death of partners did not necessarily mark the beginning of the end of a household, as families could also be reconstructed by remarriage. In the modern Western world, with historically high mean life spans, it is usually anticipated that the final stages of the life cycle of the family will see a long period of old age, during which cohabiting partners will enjoy a period of active retirement. But with the relatively high mortality that prevailed in early modern England, this pattern is likely to have been very different. The same circumstances have also been seen as having profound effects on attitudes to death, burial and memorial, all of which have been perceived as sensitive indicators of the nature of family life. Thus, the ways in which families were disrupted by death can perhaps tell us as much about family life as their formation and expansion.

WIDOWS, WIDOWERS AND ORPHANS

It has been calculated that broken families were actually more common in pre-industrial England than in even the modern United States of America. Modern Western societies tend to have high rates of separation and divorce, and while these circumstances were rare in the past, the prevailing demographic conditions meant it was unusual for both partners to live to see their children reach adulthood. Perhaps between a quarter and a half of all children lost one or both parents before the age of twenty-five [64 *pp. 160–73*]. Early modern society thus had a relatively large proportion of widows, widowers and orphans.

With no adequate social security system, no legal adoption, and no real tradition of fostering, the care of orphans was a considerable problem. Where they had been left some means, the fatherless and orphaned were often catered for through the system of guardianship. Among the aristocracy, until 1646, this was administered through a system of wardships, which could be used for profit, were able to decide the marriage of the children concerned and could be sold by the Crown. The church courts and those of some larger towns, such as London and Bristol, held a wider jurisdiction where there was an estate to be administered for a child. Guardians could and often were nominated in wills, but if this was not done, they could be appointed by the courts to look after the financial and legal aspects of parenthood. This was one instance where wider kin may have proved significant. Almost half the guardians nominated in wills from three Yorkshire parishes in the sixteenth and early seventeenth centuries were mothers, but a significant minority, nearly one-fifth, were members of the wider kinship network [97 *p. 16*].

Grandparents, in particular, were singled out by the Poor Law from 1601 as responsible where poor orphans could not work. However, given that demographic conditions made the chances of individuals surviving to see their grandchildren very low, this would have tended to be a relatively infrequent occurrence. In these circumstances, the chances were that another relative would be found, but if none were available, or willing, then the children of the poor remained a particular problem. The systems of service and apprenticeship could be, and increasingly in our period were, pressed into service for older children, but very young orphans were vulnerable. Some major urban centres had charitable institutions designed to deal with this problem, such as Christ's Hospital in London, which was founded in 1552 for orphaned and foundling (abandoned) children, who were too young to go into service. By 1634, it had reached a peak of admitting over 1,000 inmates a year [253 *pp. 69–70*]. Conditions were far from pleasant and the mortality rate was high, passing 50 per cent in some periods in the late sixteenth century. Despite this, it was never able to match the demand of the capital, let alone the country as a whole, where most children in this situation appear to have been catered for in a more informal manner. In many cases families appear to have taken such children in, in exchange for additional poor relief.

While the loss of a parent could have profound effects on the life of a child, the demise of a partner was clearly the most emotionally distressing event an individual was likely to suffer. Despite high mortality, most first marriages tended to last over twenty years, intensifying the wrench between partners when it occurred. In surveys of households between the late sixteenth and early eighteenth centuries around a fifth were headed by only one partner, suggesting that widowhood was a fairly common circumstance. Since women were, on average, two or three years younger than their husbands, there tended to be more widows than widowers, for most of our period. The financial consequences were often less of a problem for men, who usually simply continued to control their wives' financial contribution to the marriage. Women could be in a more precarious position. In the Archdiocese of York and in London they automatically received one-third of their husband's estate if there were children and half if none, but elsewhere there was the usual confusing pattern of local custom. In most cases where married men made wills, they were careful to make some provision for their wives and to ensure that any money, land or goods they left went, ultimately, to their children.

For bereaved adults, many of the same pressures that applied to marriage applied to remarriage. In addition, the survival of children from a previous marriage might make it imperative. Fathers with relatively young children (in a society where their nearest helpful kin might be some considerable distance away), particularly if they could not afford a nurse, had a serious problem. Many widowed women may have had much greater incentives in the difficulties they would encounter in providing for themselves and any children in the absence of a husband's labour, skills and connections. Women who were widowed undoubtedly gained a positive social and legal position (they, unlike married women, could hold property), which was otherwise unavailable to them, but were often on the social margins and particularly susceptible to the vicissitudes of economics [132 *pp. 227–35*]. It was probably easier for men to re-enter the marriage market, as their position as a potential partner may have been most dependent on wealth and status, which tended to increase towards the middle of the life course. Widowed women, particularly if they had children of their own, could be a less attractive prospect. Any wealth they carried with them might be earmarked for existing children, and their physical attractiveness and ability to have more children were likely to be diminished by their relative age. These circumstances partly explain why in a sample of those who could be identified as remarrying in parish registers of the seventeenth and eighteenth centuries, almost half of men but less than two-fifths of women had remarried within a year [162 *pp. 258–9*]. However, a wealthy widow could be considered a good catch and there are many examples of younger men making their fortunes by securing an estate or business through such a marriage.

The limited picture we have of these circumstances indicates that re-marriage was relatively common among both sexes. Figures for the majority of the population are difficult to determine, but among the married children of the English peerage born in the third quarter of the sixteenth century, over a third married twice [63 *p. 21*]. Rapid remarriage has been taken to indicate that there was little emotional commitment between partners. Usually, a partner was expected to mourn for at least a year. Re-marriage after that point could equally be taken to indicate that an unpleasant relationship would not have so rapidly and frequently been repeated and more significantly that the idea of marriage was an economic necessity and social norm for adults.

One result of common re-marriage was the reconstruction of families. This could become very complicated with two sets of children brought into a new household and then half-brothers and sisters born to a new couple. If a parent married more than twice, or if the new husband and wife both brought their existing children into a new household, these relationships could become intensely complex. It is clear that step-relationships were often problematic and could be acrimonious. Just as dying fathers often 'ring-fenced' inheritance for their children (to prevent it being taken over by a new marriage partner of their spouse), step-fathers would often specifically exclude their wife's children as beneficiaries. Relations between step-kin were sometimes close, but more often they tended to resent each other and the early age at which individuals tended to leave home may have seemed a blessing to those on both sides of the relationship. Nevertheless, despite their many problems, the reconstruction of family relationships shows the importance of the model of the domestic family and how vital it was to economic survival.

OLD AGE AND DISABILITY

Like youth, the existence of old age as a category in pre-industrial England is a matter of definition and debate. In a society with a relatively low mean life expectancy, we might anticipate a small proportion of the population to be elderly. Nevertheless, these figures are averages and some lived to be very old indeed. Almost a third of the population in the late seventeenth century were aged forty or more and almost one in ten were sixty or over [73 *p. 218*]. More importantly, as with youth, we need to avoid imposing our conception of what constitutes an age category and consider the ways in which the people of pre-industrial England defined their own age groups. Most significantly, unlike today, few couples experienced a period when children had left home, but during which they were able to enjoy relatively high earning power. These circumstances were largely the product of late marriage and low life expectancy. Additionally, even if they survived to see the adulthood of their children, many parents, perhaps particularly in the middling groups of society, found it was necessary to break up their holdings in order to give the next generation portions. This process of the dissolution of an estate would tend to begin relatively early, on average in the mid- to late-forties, as children began to reach maturity. As a result, the 'adult' section of the life course would normally be short and, if an individual survived, they might be increasingly dependent on others and unable to supply their own needs, which could be said to be a reasonable definition of 'old age'. The same can be said of the labouring poor, where an individual would tend to experience a decrease in their physical (and therefore earning) power from roughly the same point. In this sense, the elderly, as a group, remained a significant minority of the population, arguably more so than youth.

Partly because of late mean marriage, many elderly couples shared households with their children. In six communities for which household listings survive between 1599 and 1796, almost half of those couples aged sixty or over had one or more offspring resident with them [64 *p. 201*]. Many of these, but perhaps particularly the girls, remained or returned to look after their parents in infirmity. However, as we have already seen, it was rare for such elderly couples to share a household with a married child and his or her spouse. This suggests that these would have been the youngest children, that their marriages may have been delayed, or made less likely by these circumstances. For example, Leonard Wheatcroft, of Ashcroft in Derbyshire, whose primary employment was as a tailor, after the death of his wife in 1689, experienced both declining finances and health. He was probably cared for by his youngest daughter until in 1694, when aged nineteen, she went to act as a servant to her father's brother. At this point, his youngest son, Titus, aged about fourteen, returned from his apprenticeship as a tailor to keep house for his father for almost two years. At the end of this time, Sarah came home to help and may have stayed until her father's death in 1701. In the meantime, Wheatcroft's successful eldest son appears to have provided financial assistance and another daughter visited and brought an ointment to relieve her father's lameness. This pattern of the burden falling on the youngest children, but with some financial aid, and occasional visits from other children, may have been fairly typical, at least among the middling sort [6 *p. 192*].

However, old age was not always as harmonious as this example might lead us to suggest. As we have already seen, early modern England was, at least in theory, a patriarchal society, where status should have been based, not only on rank and gender, but also on age. However, if, unlike these other systems of social classification, greater age did not necessarily mean greater economic power, the same may be true of its social significance. The diversity of individual experiences needs to be stressed. Some continued to be active to the end of their lives, but others, by choice or because of infirmity, divested themselves of both property and responsibility. With no social security system, or pensions, such an old age was a particularly difficult prospect. Many enjoyed a pleasant retirement: others we know did not, and the loss of authority that went with property, or earning power, often created a conflict between the theory of patriarchy and the realities of ownership and ability. One example from the social elite is that of John Parton, a Worcester gentleman, who settled his house on his daughter Ann and his granddaughters and moved into only half of it. In 1632, two years before his death, he commented on how strained family relationships with the younger generation had become, noting that his daughter 'keepeth me out of my house and robbes me' [8 *p. 235*]. In these circumstances, the elderly could be reduced to the status of 'sojourners' (a term also applied to the wandering poor) within their own homes [44 *p. 105*].

At the lower end of the social scale, old age could be an even greater problem. The proportion of the population that was elderly varied across our period and between different locations. In the booming cloth towns of the West Riding of Yorkshire in the late sixteenth century, there were relatively few, but in more established areas, particularly after a period of low birth rates (such as the mid-seventeenth century), they could be a significant minority. Those over sixty made up 14 per cent of the needy in the Norwich survey of the poor in 1570 and over 30 per cent of those in Salisbury in 1625 [253 *pp. 78–9*].

The same laws that, after 1601, placed the responsibility for orphans on their grandparents, placed similar duties on children and grandchildren for their impoverished elders. However, in the opinion of Paul Slack, the impracticability of this arrangement meant that the community, rather than the family, tended to care for the elderly [253 *p. 84*]. This was carried out through parish collections, the poor box kept in every church, or, increasingly, by giving them a place in one of the local almshouses that were becoming a common feature of both rural and urban communities through our period.

As age increased, so did the likelihood that other infirmities would add to an individual's difficulties. Similar problems and solutions were needed for a relatively large number of what we would now consider to be persons with disabilities. This topic has remained remarkably under-researched outside the context of the Poor Law. Where families were more prosperous, they no doubt cared for those with both physical and mental disabilities within their own homes. Wills occasionally singled them out for attention, or ensured them a room and a bed. Many were able to make an economic contribution despite their disabilities. When these individuals were poor and unable to support themselves, 'lame, impotent . . . blind' persons were specifically listed in the acts of 1598 and 1601 for payments from local rates [253 *p. 29*]. They therefore surface in surveys of the poor and poor relief, like the two 'innocents' and the blind woman who needed relief in Gillingham in Kent in the crisis famine year of 1596 [253 *p. 64*]. Numbers of the physically disabled were swelled after a period of war, such as the late Elizabethan period and particularly after the civil wars of the mid-seventeenth century, because battle-damaged limbs were almost always removed.

Despite the aid of families and communities, infirmity frequently meant that old age and in the case of those with disabilities, life could be a desperate struggle on the fringes of society. Many were, in the end, forced to rely on begging and informal charity to survive. In itself, the fact that so many persons accused of witchcraft were relatively old and usually single is a good indication of the marginality of such individuals.

DEATH AND BURIAL

In the early modern period, death was just as common as now, but tended to come more unexpectedly and earlier. It could also be on a massive and more harrowing scale, particularly in times of famine and with outbreaks of plague. Burials are usually seen as a very reliable guide to actual mortality, since it is a process that usually cannot long be avoided. Across the year, the pattern of burials was very similar to that for baptisms. There was a peak between February and April and a fall towards July, followed by a steady rise in mortality through the year. This was partly because of the high mortality among new-born infants, which made up a considerable minority of these figures. Another obvious factor was that of temperature, with cold contributing to weakness and some forms of infection. However, this pattern looked very different in towns, and in periods of epidemic disease or famine, which tended to create more deaths in summer, when the food supply was low and some diseases thrived [73 *pp. 293–7*].

As we have seen, a mass of evidence suggests that, psychologically, our ancestors differed very little from us in the emotional impact of death, in regard to both adults and children. They may, however, have been rather better at dealing with the problem as they had more rituals, and clearly defined rites of passage, which are generally acknowledged as aiding the grieving process. There was an increasing stress on the transitory nature of life in both literature and art, and, rather than making for a morbid society, this may have helped to prepare individuals for death [Plate 6]. They also had a belief in the afterlife, which many today do not, and this must have made the consequences of high mortality ultimately less wrenching, at least after the initial and inevitable shock.

There was fear of accidental death and the shifts of fate, although this was a greater problem for the majority of the population in the medieval period, because under Catholic tradition, if unshriven (without a final confession), people's sins were counted against them in Purgatory [214]. But Catholics and Protestants alike saw the importance of making a good end. This was the *ars moriandi*: the art of dying. If circumstances allowed, this would involve the family gathering around the death-bed [206, 211]. In the medieval period, bells were rung to alert neighbours, family and friends so that they could offer comfort, aid and prayers for the dying. If there were alienated relatives, this was the period in which reconciliation could be achieved. The dying also needed to give their blessing before they departed and to demonstrate their faith in God. Since most wills were made on the death-bed, it also represented a last opportunity to influence the dying in their distribution of wealth and property. After death there was a long period of mourning, which involved the wearing of black among close family and during which certain events (such as marriages) were not conducted. The length of this period tended to vary with the closeness of kinship to the deceased. Modern psychologists tend to agree that these clearly defined rituals and processes tend to aid the mourning process, allowing individuals to come to terms with grief more effectively and more quickly.

In the medieval period, relatives also had the consolation that they could affect the fate of their loved ones after death, through prayer. It was believed that Christians went first to Purgatory, until their sins were expunged and they could move on to Heaven. Prayers for the dead would speed this process. This could be done individually, or by paying a priest to sing masses for the dead. The result of this system was that, by the beginning of the sixteenth century, English churches abounded with chantries, altars and chapels at which masses were conducted. For the poor and those dead without relatives and friends, All Souls' Day (2 November) assumed a particular importance, as general prayers guaranteed that all the dead would ultimately ascend to Heaven. At times, indulgences were also sold on behalf of the Church to speed or, as some believed, complete this process. This was the issue that sparked off the Reformation in Germany and a subsequent period of religious turmoil across Europe. One of the most visible impacts of reform on the appearance of church fabric in England, and on the idea of death, was the removal and destruction of these chantries and altars in 1547 [16 *pp. 450–64*]. The Protestant view of the after life was far more streamlined. The dead were allotted either to Heaven or Hell, and could not move between them [210 *pp. 110–30*]. The dead could be remembered, but their fate could not be affected. Some historians have characterised this as a separation of the community of the living from that of the dead. If this is an accurate assessment, it must also have meant a distancing of family members by the barrier of death [78 *pp. 465–9*]. However, even the most fervent Protestants constantly looked forward to a reunion after death or at Judgement Day.

Naturally, the period between death and burial was usually short. In summer, or where infectious disease was involved, it could be very rapid indeed. But if circumstances permitted, the body would be washed and prepared, often by the local midwife. It was then 'wound' in bands or a single cloth shroud. There was then a period in which it was 'watched', under constant attendance until the appointed time of the funeral. This was partly to ensure that the body was not tampered with, but it was also a mark of respect for the dead. During this period interested parties would visit the body, further helping them to come to terms with bereavement, particularly if they had been unable to attend the death-bed [78 *pp. 421–30*]. The body would then process to the place of burial, sometimes carried on a bier, sometimes on a horsedrawn hearse. The mourners, composed of family, friends and kin would accompany the body in a display of respect and sorrow [Plate 7]. In medieval wills, cloaks and hoods were often given to poor men to act as mourners and, although this practice disappeared at the Reformation, the poor could often expect a dole of money if they attended. Although the body would usually be carried in a coffin, often this was owned by the parish and the body would be placed in the ground in a linen and later a woollen shroud. However, the rich were buried in their own coffins and this practice expanded down the social scale throughout our period.

The rite of the medieval Church was an elaborate process of intercession for the dead, while that of the established Protestant Church emerged from the mid-sixteenth century as a commemoration of a life. This was a function emphasised by the increasing use of funeral sermons for those of high status, which dwelt on their virtues and achievements. After the ceremony a meal and drink would be provided, particularly for the chief mourners, but often, especially where the rich were concerned, for all those participating. Like marriage, burial thus remained a very public event; however, Puritan desires to limit the pomp of elaborate ceremonies may have done something to reduce participation, particularly from the mid-seventeenth century.

As we have seen, the early modern period has been percieved as one of increasing individualism in the commemoration of the dead. Lawrence Stone argued for a change from collective and unmarked burial to individual internment signified by increasingly elaborate monuments. In the medieval period, burials in church were very common. Many burials of the wealthy were marked by brasses and occasionally in stone. These were designed to remind future worshippers of the departed and to invite prayers. For this reason, these monuments were largely removed during the Reformation (with most of those that survive having been hidden and later replaced). Elaborate monuments were unpopular in some quarters during the mid- to late-sixteenth centuries, but began to make a comeback over the next fifty years, probably because they had become distanced from their implications of Catholicism. They were often not simply depictions of individuals, but also of families. Wives, occasionally in their multiples, and children were depicted. Heraldry also became common, showing the ancestry and kinship of the deceased, as did symbols of death [*Docs 21 and 22*]. However, throughout our period monuments in churches remained the preserve of a small elite.

As the population expanded, increasing proportions of the dead were buried outside the church, within the churchyard. This can be taken to indicate a separation between the living at worship and the dead, but it may simply indicate the interior was unable to cope with the number of burials. From the late eighteenth century, the use of gravestones in churchyards became increasingly common for all social classes. In fact, before this point, most graves were probably marked, but with wooden crosses which have not survived.

Some individuals were excluded from burials in churchyards. Numbered among these were some executed felons, suicides and the unbaptised. They were often placed outside the churchyard wall, or at a crossroads, marking their exclusion from the Christian community. However, these policies were far from universally applied and a blind eye was also often turned to the burial of Catholics within churchyards, a ceremony usually carried out under the cover of darkness.

Death and commemoration underwent considerable changes in this period, but it is far from certain that this fits the pattern of a shift from collective and anonymous burial to an individualistic system of marked and named resting places. Some changes indicate evolving religious ideas and needs, others reflected the massive shifts in social structure and population. While patterns of death and burial underwent a transformation, they appear to have been the result of a more complex set of causes and events than many historians have previously assumed.

Both survival and death were potential social problems in early modern England. However, people had developed and adapted social mechanisms to deal with both sets of circumstances. Such solutions often led to social and personal tensions, but they did allow society and the family to continue to function. All elements of the problems of old age and death demonstrate a reaffirmation of the family as the primary social unit for the dissemination of wealth, but also affection and companionship. The question to be answered in the remaining section of this book is the degree to which this re-creative process was forced to adapt due to long-term cultural and economic change.

PART THREE

ASSESSMENT – CONTINUITY AND CHANGE

CHAPTER TEN

THE IMPACT OF IDEAS ON FAMILY LIFE

As we have seen, less than two decades ago, it was widely accepted that the family underwent a fundamental transformation in the early modern period. This picture has altered radically and there has been tremendous stress upon continuity in the most important aspects of family life. Nevertheless, the early modern era remains one in which it is still accepted that economic, social and intellectual change did take place, even if it fails to fit the predicted pattern of class creation and modernisation that was once assumed. In the light of these circumstances, it is necessary to understand whether these factors had any impact on the experience of family life in the early modern period and, if so, what exactly that impact was. This section will attempt to look at the two major areas in which change has been perceived, the realm of ideas and that of economics.

There are a number of strands of intellectual change in our period that have, at various times, been advanced as having profound effects on the nature of family life. The first contrasts medieval ideas with the Humanism that came to prominence in English intellectual circles at the end of the fifteenth and beginning of the sixteenth centuries. The second is the Reformation, which began to affect English religion in the early to mid-sixteenth century, but was not entirely played out even at the end of our period. The third and final strand is the Enlightenment, which was just gathering speed towards the end of the eighteenth century and, arguably, did not have its most important effects until long after our period had closed. All these intellectual movements have been perceived as creating new concepts of the family and of family life. The degree to which they actually represented new ideas about society and the way and degree to which they affected the pattern of family life remain some of the most important issues in understanding this institution in our period.

HUMANISM

The Renaissance, the rediscovery of classical art and thought, which began in Northern Italy towards the end of the fourteenth century, reached its peak

in Northern Europe in the early decades of the sixteenth century. The intellectual movement associated with these ideas, usually referred to as Humanism,
stressed classical standards of scholarship and logical argument, condemning
many perceived 'abuses' in the Catholic Church. Its most famous exponent in
Northern Europe, Desiderius Erasmus (1466–1536) of Rotterdam, has also
been credited with defining a new view of aspects of family life which were
to be profoundly influential [235].

The most obvious contrast between Humanist thinking and what came
before, was its general optimism concerning human nature. This was particularly important in relation to children, as most medieval commentators had
tended to follow St Augustine's lead, stressing the concept of original sin to
a point where the new-born child was sometimes depicted as actively evil.
Following Pagan and classical writers, many Humanists side-stepped much of
the Christian theology of the medieval period. Erasmus depicted the child as
morally neutral and therefore a vessel that needed to be protected from the
contamination of the world and educated to avoid these evils [199 *p. 115*].

The process of education could also commence much earlier. Whereas
medieval commentators were almost universally agreed that children could
not be educated until they were about seven years old, Erasmus argued that
education was possible and even desirable from the earliest age. It has been
suggested that this emphasis changed the pattern of care for the young child
from the mother to the father, but, in re-emphasising maternal breast-feeding
as the beginning of this process and condemning the use of wet-nurses, Erasmus
was also attempting to reinforce the maternal bond [186 *pp. 43–4*]. It should
be pointed out that Erasmus seems to have assumed that this education should
be limited to boys; however, he also went some way to suggesting that women
had equal intellectual and moral capacities. His friend and the most famous
English Humanist of this period, Thomas More, is partly famous for having
educated his daughters to a very high level.

Additionally, Erasmus said a great deal that affected relations between
men and women. He placed considerable stress on the suitability of tempera-
ments between marriage partners, opening the possibility of perceiving marriage as a partnership, rather than a divinely ordained dictatorship. There was
also a more positive view of sexual intercourse between married partners,
always treated with reservation by the Catholic Church. Rather than being
perceived as a necessary evil, this was now a healing process and a means of
strengthening the links between them.

This positive view of marriage, added to the endorsement of female
learning and underlining of women's intellectual capacities, has been seen as
instituting a new and more positive view of women. In the words of Ralph
Houlbrooke, 'the Renaissance mounted the first serious attack on the medieval belief in women's natural inferiority in intellect and virtue and their
physiological imperfection' [33 *p. 32*]. This is not to ascribe to Humanists the

tenets of modern feminism, but they did provide a view of both women and relations between the sexes which was to be picked up by different groups and individuals across our period.

Humanism also had profound effects on the way in which family relations were depicted, both in art and literature. Its influence can be seen in classically inspired funerary monuments, which, as we have already seen, from this period began to depict the departed in greater realism. They also became much more likely to incorporate epitaphs that emphasised individual achievement as a model for the living, in the classical style. There were also classical influences that helped to change portraiture to a more realistic depiction of the living and it is from the 1520s that we begin to see paintings of family groups, starting with the Humanist household of Thomas More. Humanism influenced styles of writing, including the diary, but also the way in which letters were written, tending to encourage simpler forms of expression and terms of address.

Because Humanism helped to change the form of art and literature, it is tempting to overstate its impact. This was a problem that deceived many of the pioneers of the history of the emotions of family life. It is possible that these changes mirrored changes in feeling and affections, but it is equally possible that they simply reflect new forms and means of expressing constant values. It also is possible to push the distinctiveness of Humanism as an intellectual movement too far. Many of the elements of the picture of childhood and relationships between the sexes that Humanist writers depicted were not necessarily alien to other branches of medieval thought. One problem is that in examining Humanist writings and those of other strands of late medieval philosophy we are not comparing like with like. Surviving medieval writings on the family were usually produced by clerics for clerics, often with a pastoral or legal role in mind. This was a very different audience and intention from those commentaries and conduct books that begin to appear in the sixteenth century, which were aimed at a lay audience who had different needs and expectations [13].

It seems, then, that Humanism did represent a significantly different emphasis concerning relations between parents and children and men and women. However, the degree to which this emphasis was revolutionary, and the degree to which it simply provided new means for expression, is open to debate. There is also the question of the extent to which these shifts in intellectual thought had an impact on the daily lives of the people of England in the early modern period, an issue to which we will return at the end of this chapter.

THE REFORMATION

In recent years, the great shift in the study of religion in early modern Europe has been from theology and institutions to its reception and impact. The series of religious movements that swept across Western Europe from the second decade of the sixteenth century has been increasingly perceived as a motor of social change and historians have naturally looked to the family as an element in this pattern. Two major areas of thought have been debated for England. The first is the nature of early sixteenth-century Protestant thought compared with medieval Catholic teaching on the family. The second is the impact of Puritanism in the late sixteenth and early seventeenth centuries.

It has been argued by Steven Ozment and Lyndal Roper that the Reformation reinforced patriarchy and that Martin Luther (its founding father), in his rejection of celibacy both theologically and personally, also elevated the married state to a higher level [229, 231]. He and his followers were clearly keen to state that the patriarchal system was to be pre-eminent. Fathers were to rule their wives and children, just as magistrates ruled their towns and provinces. They were also keen to bury clerical celibacy and monastic religious orders by stating that marriage was not only a 'hospital' for lust, where it could be properly contained, but a higher state, inspired by God.

One problem is that in their emphasis on patriarchy, Luther and his followers may simply have been restating medieval ideas about family life. What may be significantly different is the fact that in the sixteenth century they would be expressed so often and in a climate of social disruption. In this atmosphere, all parties, Protestants and Catholics alike, were tempted to clamp down on any perceived threat to the patriarchal system.

Also, particularly in England, Protestantism owed much to Humanism, perhaps especially in the area of family life. Kathleen Davis, in her study of literary advice on marriage, pointed to the continuity between what she characterised as 'medieval Catholic' and 'later Protestant' advice on areas such as adultery, relationships between husband and wife and patriarchy [224]. Patrick Collinson, however, noted that the advice she had described as 'medieval' was in fact from early sixteenth-century Humanist handbooks and this supports the view that the watershed in ideas was between medieval Catholicism and Humanism and not between Catholicism and Protestantism [13]. Both reforming movements drew on classical and biblical precedents and, not surprisingly, came to very similar conclusions. One of the most influential writers on marriage, the Swiss reformer Heinrich Bullinger, made considerable use of Erasmus, and was himself much quoted, emulated and copied by English writers [224 *p. 80*]. This link is so marked that it has been argued that 'Protestantism can be seen as ensuring the continuance of the Christian Humanist tradition' [53 *p. 43*].

What has been assumed of Protestantism has been particularly applied to Puritanism, the more radical branch of reformed religion that came to prominence in England from the late sixteenth to the mid-seventeenth centuries. In 1969, Levin L. Schücking presented the image of the Puritan family as a unit separated off from general society, introspectively focusing on the Bible and their place among God's elect [234] [Plate 4]. Schücking's ideas were particularly significant because it was felt that Puritan attitudes were those which became dominant, not only in modern England but also in North America. This thesis was expanded by other authors, including Christopher Hill, who examined the spiritualisation of the household [226].

In many ways, Puritan ideas were very similar to those of other religious groups and tendencies. They all shared an emphasis on patriarchy and companionate marriage. However, there were some areas where Puritans did differ significantly from their contemporaries. A number of these we have encountered throughout this book. Most importantly, they tended to have a more elevated view of marriage. Naturally, Catholics, having retained clerical celibacy and religious orders, usually saw celibacy as a higher state. But the same tendency can be detected in the works of conservative Protestants in England, who like Richard Hooker in 1594, saw the single life as 'a thing more angellicall and divine' [53 *p. 39*]. Puritans also disliked the institution of godparenthood and generally disapproved of elaborate public ceremonial, arguably making the family the emphasis of a smaller familial circle. Elsewhere, they may have differed significantly, not so much in their opinions, as in the ferocity with which they pursued these views. The particular condemnation of the double standard evident in Puritan polemic can be seen as a result of a view of sex as a positively good thing within marriage. This element has, controversially, been seen as a factor in the development of a more tolerant attitude to women, which expressed itself in the extreme sects that emerged in the mid-seventeenth century, a number of which had women as leading figures and even preachers [223]. However, there was another side to such ideas. Most obviously, Puritans were far harsher in their attitude to sex outside marriage. The ultimate expression of this view was the notorious Adultery Act of 1650, brought by the Puritan regime that followed victory in the civil wars, which made it, and incest, capital offences [149].

Regarding general attitudes to women, the more optimistic view of their educational abilities evident in Humanism had also survived in literate circles within English Protestantism. It is evident from time to time in the seventeenth century in works of a relatively radical bent, such as *The Women's Sharpe Revenge*, published in 1640, but also in conservative tracts like Mary Astel's *A Serious Proposal to the Ladies*, published in 1697, but these remained highly contested views and it is less than certain that they had a wider impact on the place of women in society.

THE ENLIGHTENMENT

The Enlightenment was a rationalist movement with roots in the seventeenth century, but which began to dominate intellectual thinking in the eighteenth. It rejected many aspects of formal religion, often substituting deism or even atheism, and ultimately became linked to the 'Scientific Revolution' that has been seen as taking place from the eighteenth century. This movement is often seen as the origin of modern intellectual thought, having profound effects on ideas about the universe, men, women and society. It has also been depicted as making important alterations to a number of areas that affect the nature of family life, including childhood, sexuality, morality and women.

If Erasmus marked the beginnings of a shift to a view of children as morally neutral, Jean Jacques Rousseau's *Émile*, published in 1762, is often credited as the first work that depicted the child as inherently good, later to be corrupted by the influence of society. Rousseau may not have been the first to draw attention to childhood, but he is often credited with being among the first to attempt to investigate it as a separate state, and not simply an annex to adult life. He adopted a very different approach from that which had dominated literate thinking from the Renaissance, substituting emphasis on education for an intention to leave young children to their childhood, learning from nature and not from man. Tutors, if they could not be avoided, were to be facilitators not dictators. It is possible to recognise in these ideas debates that have come to dominate thinking on education into the present century.

However, as is often the case, it is possible to overstate Rousseau's originality. More positive ideas on childhood also have a longer history and he owed much to the 'piece of clean paper' approach to childhood, attributed to John Locke's *Some Thoughts on Education*, published in 1693 [*Doc. 23*]. Here it was argued that children were born, like animals, without a moral sense and therefore must be forced to obey, but later would develop both will and conscience and had to be treated accordingly. Similarly, the two ideas for which Rousseau usually receives most credit, his opposition to swaddling and wet-nursing, were also not his. Locke had already expressed doubts about swaddling and, as we have already seen, the employment of wet-nurses was questioned from at least the sixteenth century. In these respects, the Enlightenment in England did not mark the beginnings of new ideas about childhood and childcare, but the intensification and wider distribution of existing ideas.

A similar pattern can be seen in Enlightenment thinking about sexuality. The picture drawn by one of the most important pioneers in this area, Michel Foucault, is of a growing interest in sex in the eighteenth century, which derived from the beginnings of modern medicine and the science of the mind [225]. This was reflected in learned texts, the beginnings of an understanding of the human body and, for the first time, a shift away from the erroneous assumptions of Aristotle concerning the female reproductive system, on which, frighteningly, much medical practice had previously been based [Plate 1]. It can also be seen, so it is argued, in the explosion of sexual literature and artistic representations of pornography that were a feature of the late eighteenth century.

The way in which women's sexuality was perceived has been seen as changing in the Enlightenment, from that of women as sexually active (and therefore dangerous) to being perceived as purely neutral, with men as the active (or over-active) element. This has been used in part to explain the disappearance of witchcraft accusations, as women moved from the sexually charged and potentially destructive witch to the bland heroines of novels like Richardson's *Pamela*. Attitudes to homoeroticism have also been seen as changing with a new medical concern over 'unnatural relations between men'.

However, the scientific basis of the Enlightenment in these areas was strictly limited. For example, there was a virtual panic in the eighteenth century over the effects of masturbation, because it was believed that personal physical, and even national decay, would inevitably follow the waste of so much semen [233 *p. 3*]. The explanation of a decline in witchcraft prosecutions is rather unconvincing, since they had virtually disappeared across Europe by the end of the seventeenth century, and in England were in decline before the end of the sixteenth. It should also be pointed out that homosexuality was just as abhorrent to the moral community in the sixteenth and seventeenth centuries as it was to be in the eighteenth and nineteenth. Finally, the boom in sexual literature and pornography is perhaps better evidence of wider literacy and less effective censorship.

A greater claim for originality can be made for another famous aspect of Enlightenment thinking, that affecting sexual morality. We have already noted that medieval and Humanist authors, but particularly Protestants influenced by Calvin, were almost universal in their condemnation of the double standard. In contrast, this is a concept many major thinkers in the eighteenth century actually appear to have embraced. Many literate men felt able to write about their numerous affairs in a way that would have been unacceptable previously. For example, Samuel Johnson argued that good wives would turn a blind eye to their husband's philandering [233 *p. 5*].

Another area where the Enlightenment does appear to have seen the emergence of a new and important strand in intellectual thinking, is that of attitudes to women. Many Enlightenment figures were very pessimistic about the abilities of women. They tended to re-emphasise the traditional line on their subjugation to men. Rousseau himself stated that 'the woman is made to please the man' and that she 'is always subordinate to man' and learning in a woman is 'unpleasing and unnecessary'. This was exemplified by the character of Sophie who acted as an inferior counterpart to Émile [55 *p. 358*]. Nevertheless, what emerged in the eighteenth century was a remarkable level of polemic written by women that argued for their intellectual and even social equality [*Doc. 24*]. This was in part built upon the foundation left by Humanist and Protestant thinking about women's education, but it was able to advance partly because of the contradiction evident in much Enlightenment thinking between human rights and the position of women. The obvious example is the tract by Mary Wollstonecraft, *Vindication of the Rights of Women*, written in 1792, which extended the ideas Thomas Paine had set forth in the *The Rights of Man* [230 *pp. 7–32*]. It should not be assumed that these ideas were widely accepted – they were strongly argued against in many intellectual circles and probably lacked popular appeal – but nevertheless they were to prove an important foundation for later intellectual and social change in this aspect of social and family life.

THEORY AND PRACTICE

Most of the evidence that we have for intellectual change comes in writings by and for a tiny social elite. Even where contrasts of thought or emphasis between different intellectual groups can be identified, it is necessary to explain how, and to what extent, these ideas were spread throughout society. One means by which these ideas could have reached wider acceptance is through the mechanisms of social control, which included the Church and the law. Another is by cultural means, such as discussion, public lectures and the rapidly expanding use of print.

In religion, the Reformation was promulgated by two major media, preaching and the written word. The former was theoretically forced on everyone and the latter was available to an increasing proportion of the population. Changes in law might have had their effects, but the most dramatic changes appeared to have floundered when they became unacceptable to the majority of the population. The legislation simplifying religious ritual or attempting to clamp down on illicit activity was overturned for the majority in the early 1660s, and much of it, most obviously the Adultery Act, was already a dead letter before that point. The Act itself resulted in virtually no prosecutions, perhaps because of an unwillingness of citizens to see their neighbours hanged for such offences, but also because proof in law was virtually impossible. The few women who did act as religious leaders in the English Civil War, had also largely disappeared from view by 1660. As they became more organised and searched for greater respectability, the majority of sects upheld the patriarchal system through their systems of discipline. It is perhaps most significant that later feminists never looked back to this period as one of liberty from patriarchy [223 p. 210]. Most of the reforms brought in by Puritans, either as a pressure group or government, were short-lived or of limited impact, and failed to have a lasting effect on the population in general. Whatever challenge had been presented by non-conformity had definitely been seen off by the time of the Restoration.

The Renaissance and the Enlightenment present a similar set of problems. The first was of more limited scope, being highly dependent on literary works, often published in Latin and accessible only to a tiny minority of the population. In contrast, recent historians have tended to stress the social context of the Enlightenment. The massive increase in publishing and expansion of literacy, the importance of visual representations, new institutions like public lectures, lending libraries and coffee houses, all helped in the process of spreading ideas from elite to popular culture. However, the actual spread of ideas on family life itself is difficult to chart. We know that some of the nobility, gentry and middling sort owned or read books written in French about child care, and even attempted to put their ideas into practice. But there is little evidence of these ideas gradually being spread through the English written record. As Lawrence Stone admitted, although many English commentaries on childhood and education were influenced by Rousseau's ideas, many others remained steadfastly old-fashioned in their suggestions well into the nineteenth century [55 *pp. 424–5*] [Plate 5]. Most problematically, the ideas of sexual liberty put forward by some writers never became widely accepted and the sexual attitudes of the nineteenth century look far more like that of Puritan advice writers than the men of letters of the Enlightenment.

The only way of proving that these movements had an effect on actual practice is to find elements within them that appear to have a measurable impact on behaviour in family life. Such evidence is naturally very difficult to produce, but claims have been made for the practices of swaddling and wet-nursing. Anecdotal evidence has been taken to suggest that swaddling declined as a practice from the seventeenth century. Swaddled children began to disappear from funerary monuments from this point. Rousseau himself suggested that it was 'almost obsolete' in England in 1762 [55 *p. 424*]. Similarly, the dramatic fall in infant mortality among members of the aristocracy, by around 30 per cent in the third quarter of the eighteenth century, has been taken as clear evidence of a fall in the practice [56 *pp. 187–233*].

However, the timing of both these sets of changes is problematic. Swaddling was not much condemned, and even widely encouraged, before the last decade of the seventeenth century, but appears to have begun to die out before this point. In contrast, wet-nursing had been almost universally attacked by every commentator writing from the beginning of the fifteenth century, but apparently survived to decline rapidly in the last quarter of the eighteenth century. The disjunction between the content of writing and the actions of even the social elite is obvious, and has not, as yet, been satisfactorily explained.

Although shifts and changes in practice can be seen as results of major intellectual movements, they do not form a linear pattern; conflicting systems of thought existed side by side. New ideas do not necessarily come to dominate and what does appear to command attention are those ideas that are acceptable to the existing cultural values of the population. It seems that changing ideas could have a considerable impact on the experience of family life, but this does not necessarily mean that they indicate different conceptions of childhood, gender or the family. Rather they appear to have marked the same attitudes and ideas in different contexts.

CHAPTER ELEVEN

ECONOMIC CHANGE

The process of industrialisation, which is usually thought to have begun in the second half of the eighteenth century, has traditionally been seen as a major watershed in the social history of England. However, it is now widely accepted that many of the important trends of this period had a much longer history, stretching back into the early modern era. These processes began to transform England from an agricultural and rural society, into an industrial and predominately urban one. There were alterations to agriculture, increases in manufactured output and important changes in the structure of populations through evolving patterns of migration and a growth of some important towns. Although it is now rare for historians to speak in stark terms of a shift from one family form to another, the possibility remains that these changes may have had a profound impact on the nature of family life. This chapter will examine three aspects of this pattern: the shifts in landholding that helped transform the social structure of early modern society, the changes in methods and volumes of manufacturing which predated industrialisation and the movement to the towns which accompanied these phenomena.

PROLETARIANIZATION

As we have already seen, in the early sixteenth century in the majority of English rural communities, where mixed pastoral and agrarian agriculture predominated, there were relatively large numbers of small farmers, usually calling themselves husbandmen, who owned a few acres that formed a mainstay of their economic support. By the end of the seventeenth century, this strata had almost disappeared to be replaced by a slightly enlarged grouping of wealthy farmers, often describing themselves as yeomen, and a much larger section of poor rural labourers, who appeared to own little or no agricultural land. This process is usually referred to as 'proletarianization', because in Marxist theory these groups would form the proletariat or working class in industrialisation.

Traditionally, this pattern of social division was blamed on enclosure (a process by which common land and the sub-divided holdings of the medieval

strip system were claimed and partitioned by large landholders for more efficient agriculture) and engrossing (by which smaller farms were combined to
produce more viable holdings) [23 *pp. 137–8, 173–80*] [Plate 8]. However,
the impact of these changes in land use in the sixteenth and early seventeenth
centuries pales into insignificance beside the parliamentary enclosure of the
late eighteenth century, long after this process of social division had been
completed in most of lowland England. It therefore is likely that the cause was
the relatively high inflation of the period, which reduced the viability of small-
holdings, forcing their sale, while the more successful farmers were able to
buy up much of this land, increasing the size of their estates and allowing them
to make their agriculture more efficient. It may also have been exacerbated by
the related factor of increasing population, which meant that resources had to
be sub-divided between larger numbers of children to a point where they ceased
to be viable. As a result, they were sold to ensure survival and the former small-
holders and their descendants were forced to rely on their labour for income.

The results of these events on family life were profound. As the period
progressed, the implication is that fewer and fewer men would have been
undertaking agricultural activities on their own behalf. Instead of generating
agricultural produce, then consuming, bartering or selling it, their role would
have been to undertake labour for another in exchange for wages, often on a
daily basis. In a rural context, this would have been a large farmer or estate
owner. This shifted economic power across the life course. As we have already
seen, landowners tended to have the greatest resources towards the middle of
their life course, but landless labourers were at their peak of earning power in
young manhood. What is more, the landless had no incentive to postpone
marriage until they had acquired sufficient resources to establish a viable
household through savings and inheritance. This has been seen as weaken-
ing the links between generations, as the economic significance and control
of parents lessened. Furthermore, younger generations would now have had
every incentive to marry early and have as many children as possible because
they were a potential source of income. Thus, the collapse of the systems of
life cycle service, and the fall in mean ages at marriage which occurred towards
the end of our period, can be seen as direct consequences of proletarianization
and can be argued to amount to a fundamental change in the demographic
pattern of English society.

This pattern can also be seen to have had profound effects on the economic
roles of women and children. As we have already seen, the wages of labourers
were rarely sufficient to sustain a household and as this social group grew, the
economic role of women outside the family was likely to become more important. Alice Clark argued that proletarianization destroyed the economic and
domestic partnership of men and women on the smallholding. First men then
women worked away from the home and this caused a significant deteriora-
tion in status. This was acute in the latter case, as the pay of women tended to

be lower. Appealing as this picture may be, we must, however, consider the differences in social structure that mean it did not apply across the population. Moreover, it is obvious that proletarianization did not occur evenly across the county, but affected different social, economic and geographically located groups at different rates and to different degrees. Thus, women and men did maintain a domestic, economic partnership on the land in some circumstances, for example in the families of rural yeoman farmers. They also retained an internal domestic role in some areas where there was need or place for them in the workforce. This pattern of change was also far from new. In the late medieval period when population was falling, women have been seen as enjoying something of a golden age in terms of participation in the workforce [128, 133]. Finally, much of the manufacturing work that was undertaken by women was still pursued within the home. For example, in the Bedfordshire village of Cardington in 1782, some two-thirds of housewives were engaged in a form of handicraft such as spinning or lace-making [19 *p. 58*].

A similar situation can be seen with children, who, as we have noted, have been seen as a potential source of income in the proletarianized family. It is therefore not surprising to find evidence of even relatively young children beginning to be seen employed outside the family in manufacturing processes. Famously, in the eighteenth century, Daniel Defoe noted children as young as four employed in the textile regions of England [*Doc. 26*]. Nevertheless, although many children did enter the workforce as industrialisation developed, in most of the period they would have tended to be somewhat older and, as with women, there were some social groups and processes that offered little opportunity for their employment.

It is evident that proletarianization could have profound effects on family life. It not only altered the shape of the life cycle, and with it the demographic regime of early modern England, but it also adjusted the relationships and roles within families. It also had other important implications that are associated with the essential problem of the location of this emerging social stratum. With far fewer ties to the land, it is to be expected that these social groups were highly mobile. Naturally, they tended to gravitate to where the opportunities for employment were greatest. The possibilities for relocation in 'close' parishes were often very limited, both in terms of economic opportunity and social control. As a result, rapid growth is often associated with 'open' parishes, where land could be claimed for building and economic opportunities were greater. Many open parishes were located in the highland regions of the country, while similar opportunities existed in some developing towns, particularly outside their limits in the suburbs. The result was a shift in the balance of population, away from close to open and some urban parishes and, as a result, from the South and East towards the West and North of the country. As we will see, the different circumstances prevailing in these areas also had potentially profound effects on family life.

PROTO-INDUSTRIALISATION

Industrialisation can be roughly defined as a process of manufacture dependant on technological innovation and the division of labour with a factory system. It is also often associated with a process of technological change that increased efficiency through the use of new sources of power and machines that allowed mass production. These conditions cannot accurately be said to have existed in England on a significant scale before the second half of the eighteenth century. Nevertheless, historians have argued that before this transformation of the economic landscape there were processes of production that can be identified as 'proto-industrial', which were similar in what they manufactured, but lacked these organisational and technological aspects [250, 251]. A good example is early modern woollen production, which produced both raw wool and cloth, but which, by the sixteenth century, occurred largely in the context of rural households within or close to areas of widespread sheep-farming, such as Lancashire and the West Riding of Yorkshire. Within these households, tasks were divided between different members of the family. Children often carded the wool to place all the fibres in the same direction. Women carded, but also spun the wool into thread. Finally, men often worked a handloom to make the thread into cloth. This was without the widespread use of water power and steam-driven mills that were to dominate the industrial landscape of the nineteenth century. They also lacked the mechanical spinning machines and looms that would make the textile factory the place of extreme noise and dirt. As a result, such production was not only limited in scope, but also highly labour intensive.

The areas where this pattern was clearest were those 'upland' regions of England concentrated in the North and West. In the far northern counties of Northumberland and County Durham, small-scale mining, particularly of coal, was significant, while in the far West, in Cornwall and Devon, it tended to be the rare metals of tin and copper. In southern Lancashire, and particularly in the West Riding of Yorkshire, textile weaving predominated. In South Yorkshire and the West Midlands metalworking was the most significant manufacturing sector, and 'nailer', 'cutler', 'scissorsmith' and 'scythsmith' were common occupational descriptions. However, there were other manufacturing employments across the country. In the East Midlands, it was often hosiery and shoemaking. In East Anglia and around the Wash, reed weaving was not uncommon [254]. Finally, throughout these regions there were pockets of other industries, such as woollen weaving at Haddon in Northamptonshire and Banbury in Oxfordshire [19 *pp. 39–40*].

It would also be wrong to characterise all this activity as indicating workers continually engaged in manufacturing. Many, perhaps most, of those undertaking these tasks also took part in agricultural work, either on their own behalf, or as paid labourers and the proportions of time spent on each activity could vary from individual to individual and season to season. There were some advantages to this mode of living, not least as Joan Thirsk has argued, that if misfortune attended one activity, there was always the other to fall back on [254]. These potential problems included failed harvests or fluctuations in market conditions. However, unlike agriculture, variations in markets for goods could be extreme and long lasting, as was the case, for example, in the collapse of European trade because of warfare in the 1630s. As a result, those proto-industrial workers who did not have alternative sources of income, could be much more adversely affected by circumstances than their agricultural counterparts. The effect of proletarianization meant that there were far more labourers who had no alternative source of income and in these circumstances suffering could be extreme. As one observer put it in 1677, 'they are only preserved from starving while they work; when age, sickness and death comes, themselves, their wives or their children are most commonly left on the parish' [23 *p. 139*].

It is necessary to distinguish between those who undertook this manufacturing activity on their own behalf and those who were employed in a system of 'putting-out', where a wealthy individual invested money in raw materials and paid for finished items. The workers involved in such a system would be saved the initial outlay on, for example, a loom and raw wool, and to an extent did not need the same skills, since patterns of finished items could be produced for them to copy. As a result, proto-industrialisation appears to have intensified the impact of proletarianization upon the process of family formation. Where such employment was available, the need for saving and the acquiring of skills through apprenticeship before marriage could be considered no longer applied, thus further eroding the system of service and late marriage that had previously dominated [249]. However, the main function of such a system was to increase the profits for those in charge and to reduce the control and gains for those who became the outworkers. The evidence also suggests that such organised patterns of investment and control were becoming more common through our period.

Historians have been keen to differentiate between the related processes of proletarianization and proto-industrial expansion, but they shared some important effects. Both helped to remove control of the mode of production from the hands of the majority, who increasingly ceased to be independent workers and became mere employees in a wider enterprise. They were thus dependent on wages and subject to the fluctuations of an increasingly unstable economic environment. Particularly at such times, the elderly and disabled may have become more of a burden. This created greater hardship and it has been argued that this resulted in a greater tendency to take drastic measures to reduce family size, for example through infanticide and child abandonment.

However, it has also been suggested that, in a reversal of original expectations, households that were more complex began to emerge as relatives huddled together for economic survival in times of hardship, or at those points of the life cycle when families were under particular stress. David Levine found this 'huddling' to be a feature of the decline of framework knitting in the parish of Shepshed in Leicestershire [83]. The result was that families could take on a form seemingly very similar to the much-debated peasant stem family, with parents and their married children even sharing households. However, this was not part of a life cycle system that saw property and households gradually shift from one generation to the next. Instead, it was economic desperation that forced families to break what appears to have been a common rule in family life in the past and combine two households in the hope of increasing their chances of survival.

Unfortunately, the ways in which these households functioned is almost unknown to us, and it is possible that the sources that would allow us to investigate them in detail simply do not exist for what were some of the poorest groups in society. However, examples of similar behaviour from later periods suggest that the older generation may have taken on many of the domestic tasks normally associated with women, including housework and childcare. This allowed the members of younger generations to try to make the best of their labour skills outside the household. Again, we need not assume too rosy a view of these occasional 'extended' families. Because relatives lived under the same roof does not mean that they necessarily formed positive relationships, and logic suggests that, particularly where widely accepted principles of household formation and social roles were being overturned, they were likely to be quite the opposite. What is more, given these conditions and the fact that these were the groups in society that had the highest rates of mortality, it seems that such relationships were likely to be very short-lived.

URBANISATION

In 1500 only around 10 per cent of the population of England and Wales lived in towns of over 3,000 inhabitants; by 1750 the proportion had almost doubled. This amounted to a significant restructuring of the population of the country, but this expansion was very uneven. Perhaps half of the inhabitants of large towns lived in London. It housed around 60,000 people in 1500, 200,000 by 1600, passing 700,000 by the end of our period, making it the largest city in Europe [242]. What is more, between the mid-seventeenth and mid-eighteenth centuries, perhaps one in six of the population lived in the capital at some point in their lives [256]. Although London dominated, regional centres, such as Bristol and Warwick, shared similar rates of expansion, while places like Sheffield, which were little more than villages at the beginning of our period, began to grow prodigiously towards the end. Much of this expansion was possible because of migration, particularly into unregulated suburbs, like those in the East End of London, also transforming the shape and nature of the urban experience [*Doc. 25*].

The nature of the process of urbanisation was partly the product of the two economic processes we have already examined. The landless labourers created by proletarianization often tended to gravitate towards towns to find employment, because begging was more successful, or because urban centres had systems of charity and thus suggested more likelihood of economic survival. However, the rate at which this drift to the towns occurred was probably slowed, rather than speeded up, by the rise of proto-industrial production. Particularly in the first part of our period, there was a drift of manufacturing away from towns, perhaps partly because of the restrictive controls of gilds and civic authorities. The often perceived decline of the regulatory ability of these institutions and the introduction of new areas of manufacture meant that in the eighteenth century economic development ceased to be a break on urban expansion and became an accelerator. As proto-industrialisation was replaced by full industrialisation towards the end of our period, there was a decisive shift towards factory production that was often located in towns, both old and new. That is not to say that this occurred in all urban centres. Some, like Norwich, York and Bedford, which had all been significant towns in the medieval and throughout the early modern periods (although they saw some generally lighter industrial employments), were more significant as social centres and local markets, and therefore expanded at a slower rate. Some established towns, such as Bristol, Coventry and Leicester, became important industrial centres, as did newer towns such as Birmingham, Leeds or Manchester. This was not the only form of employment within them and well beyond our period factory work accounted for a minority of the workers within even the most significant industrial towns.

In addition, the impact of the factory system on family life has been called into question. Given our knowledge of the lack of peasant stem families in early modern England, it is no longer possible to suggest that the factory cut the young off from their parents. In fact, age at leaving home may actually have risen for factory workers. As married women, contrary to many expectations, rarely participated in the industrial work force, it did not often rob children of their mothers and destroy this crucial family bond. This meant that there was a clear division of labour between the husband working away from home and the mother largely within and around it, but, as we have already seen, this division had existed, with varying degrees of intensity, since the medieval period.

If industrialisation did not necessarily mark a watershed in the nature of family life, it is clear that the associated urbanisation, a process that, as we have seen, was occurring throughout our period, did have some obvious effects on family life. Firstly, the relatively high mortality of the period was extreme in the densely packed conditions of the early modern town. High local mobility to and from towns usually ensured involvement in national outbreaks of infectious disease, most obviously the bubonic plague before the mid-1660s, but accompanied by a whole host of different epidemics of lesser impact. High population density and the particularly unpleasant lack of hygiene in towns (which had no closed sewers or refuse collection and had to deal with uniquely large quantities of general, human and animal waste) tended to ensure the spread of plague, along with the associated dangers of typhus, dysentery and cholera. Furthermore, in times of harvest failure, urban dwellers tended to suffer the most, as rural populations, lacking a surplus, would fail to supply them. Infant mortality was particularly high, often exceeding 200 per 1,000 live births and some large towns could only maintain their size through a large-scale process of continual migration, leading to highly unstable populations [242 *pp. 85–90*].

Traditionally, this process of urbanisation has been seen as destroying links between the family and both traditional communities and distant relatives. However, there is considerable evidence that urbanization, like proto-industrialisation, could actual invert this model. For Preston in the nineteenth century, Michael Anderson found that industrial workers tended to live together in more complex households, highly dependent on each other for contact and survival, often resulting in higher proportions of more distant kin sharing residence [237]. There are indications that this was not a function of industrial society, but that urbanisation produced similar effects in early modern England. The work of Peter Clark on migrants to Kentish towns, suggests that relatives may have been particularly significant as points of entry into urban life, often continuing to act as a focus for housing and employment [240]. We have already seen how the higher mortality associated with urban environments may have forced individuals to rely on more distant relatives after the death of members of the nuclear family. However, it should be noted that although urbanisation might have affected the relationships between households and short-term patterns of residence, there is little evidence that urban society possessed distinctly different patterns of household structure before the end of our period.

Urbanisation also had other effects on family life. Although it would be wrong to idealise the cottages of the rural poor, the conditions of urban poverty were inevitably more unpleasant because housing was bound to be at a premium. The drift to the towns unavoidably increased the numbers of urban poor. This, in turn, placed particular stresses on family economics, a problem often only resolved through begging, theft or prostitution. In times of recession, proto-industrial workers in towns were the most vulnerable, as they could rarely fall back on agriculture as a source of income. They were also, of course, one of the most densely concentrated groups and in times of crisis their ranks would often be swelled by incoming rural poor from the hinterland of a town, hoping to utilise the more sophisticated systems of poor relief that tended to exist in urban centres. The result was often that the local authorities were simply overwhelmed and conditions became acute. The effects of urban-isation were thus twofold, with an increase of the importance of more distant kin, but a consequent decrease in the security and standards of living. As a result, many had to raise and maintain families in urban poverty or squalor, a circumstance that became increasingly common as towns emerged as major centres of employment in the industrialised economy of the following century.

It seems that a complex set of economic changes did have a profound impact on the nature of family lives of many in this period. The collapse of the system of life cycle service, late marriage and low fertility, and the rise in population that became a feature of English society in the eighteenth century, can all be attributed to such a process. What is more, proto-industrial production provided an economic system that could accommodate much of this wage-dependent population and provided a vital bridge to the more rapid industri-alisation that began towards the end of our period. However, important as these changes were, it is still unclear whether these amounted to a fundamen-tal shift in the nature of the family or whether they were simply adjustments within an intrinsically stable system, and this will form the theme of the final chapter of this book.

CHAPTER TWELVE

THE FAMILY AND KINSHIP IN PERSPECTIVE

Understanding the scale of the impact of the changes to family life depends in part on the definition of the family and returns us to the differing methodologies outlined at the beginning of this book. However, even within the major strands of thinking about these issues, the pattern is less than clear, with suggestions of both continuity and change.

If we examine kinship, we can see that transformations in economic circumstances could have profound effects on the nature of relationships with more distant kin. Nevertheless, it is clear that in its essentials the kinship system remained unchanged. What appears to have occurred is an employment of that system where it became necessary for survival. One feature of the English kinship system is the very large numbers and range of kin that it created. Most of the time they were not called upon, but when circumstances removed other systems of support they could be, and often were, turned to for aid.

Turning to the life cycle and economy of the family, it is evident that there are similar problems. Changing economic circumstances radically adjusted the way in which most families functioned as economic units and their relationships to production and consumption. The pattern of the life cycle of the family was adapted, with the loss of much of the life cycle service that appears to have been so common in the early part of our period and a shift to earlier marriage for the majority. But in its essentials, the process of household formation remained. In most cases, marriage was still the cornerstone on which households and new generations were built. The life cycle was stretched, but not broken, by economic change in the early modern period.

With residence and reproduction, the answers remain contradictory. Firstly, the pattern of residence (except in reference to servants) seems to have remained extremely stable. However, the study of demographic trends is the area in which the clearest changes can be seen. Again, what is suggested by the evidence is that adaptation of demographic patterns was possible, while the essential framework of residence remained unchanged.

Finally, this pattern can be applied to perhaps the most difficult area of study, that of the problem of the emotions and culture of family life. Perhaps pioneers in this field were in error in assuming that changes in ideas about the family necessarily meant that there were changes in the emotional response of humans to those around them. Instead, what seems to have occurred is the expression of the same emotional values in very different circumstances, both intellectual and economic.

It seems, then, that while the family was subject to considerable economic and cultural change in the early modern period, these changes, although they impacted on the quality and experience of family life, were not of a magnitude that undermined the fundamental principles upon which it depended. Rather, what is evident is the flexibility of ideas, structures, processes and systems of family and kinship, to allow considerable variation within this framework. In this sense, one reason family life could change and vary in the early modern period was because these systems allowed considerable flexibility and adaptation. Thus, the strength of the early modern family system was in its elasticity. To adapt a common early modern metaphor, it was a branch that did not break, because it could bend.

PART FOUR · DOCUMENTS

The Pastons were a prominent noble family from Norfolk, who had some fringe involvement in the Wars of the Roses. Their letters are among the first below the rank of royalty to survive in any numbers and form one of the most extensive and detailed collections of private correspondence from before the seventeenth century. This letter contains some concerns that appear very modern.

To my well-beloved son Sir John Paston

I greet you well, and send you God's blessing and mine, letting you wit that I have received a letter from you the which ye delivered to Master Roger at Lynn, whereby I conceive that ye did think ye did not well that ye departed hence without my knowledge. Wherefore I let you wit I was right evil paid with you. Your father thought, and thinketh yet, that I was assented to your departing, and that hath caused me to have great heaviness. I hope he will be your good father hereafter, if ye demean you well and do as ye owe to do to him; and I charge you upon my blessing that in anything touching your father that should be his worship, profit, or avail, that ye do your devoir and diligent labour to the furtherance therein, as ye will have my good will; and that shall cause your father to be better father to you.

It was told me ye sent him a letter to London. What the intent thereof was I wot not, but though he took it but lightly, I would ye should not spare to write him again as lowly as ye can, beseeching him to be your good father, and send him such tidings as beth in the country there ye beth in; and that ye beware of your expense better [than] ye have be before this time, and be your own purse-bearer. I trow ye shall find it most profitable to you.

I would ye should send me word how ye do, and how ye have cherished for yourself sin ye departed hence, by some trusty man, and that your father have no knowledge thereof. I durst not let him know of the last letter that ye wrote to me, because he was so sore displeased with me at that time.

Item, I would ye should speak with Wykes and know his disposition to Jane Walsham. She hath said, sin he departed hence, but she might have him she would never [be] married; her heart is sore set on him. She told me that he said to her that there was no woman in the world he loved so well. I would not he should jape her, for she meaneth good faith; and if he will not have her let me weet not in haste, and I shall purvey for her in other wise.

As for your harness and gear that ye left here, it is in Daubeney's keeping. It was never removed sin your departing, because that he had not the keys, I trow it shall appear, but if it be take heed at betimes. Your father knoweth not where it is. I sent your grey horse to Ruston to the farrier, and he saith he shall never be naught to road, neither right good to plough or to cart. He saith he was splayed, and his shoulder rent from the body. I wot not what to do with him.

Your grandmam would fain hear some tidings from you. It were well to do that ye sent a letter to her how ye do, as hastily as ye may. And God have you in his keeping, and make you a good man, and give you grace to do as well as I would ye should do. Written at Caister the Tuesday before Saint Edmund the King.

Your Mother, M. Paston

I would ye should make much of the parson [of] Filby, the bearer hereof, and make him good cheer if ye may.

[2], pp. 99–101.

DOCUMENT 2   **THE NOTEBOOK OF NEHEMIAH WALLINGTON, 1625–26**

Wallington (1598–1658) was a turner from Eastcheap in London and the first person of relatively humble origins to leave us an extensive account of his life. The following extracts deal with the deaths of two of his children.

Elizabeth, aged 2, 1625
And about eight o'clock at night [my] wife was in the kitchen washing of dishes, my daughter being merry went unto her mother and said unto her, 'what do you here, my wife?' And at night when we were abed, says she to me, 'father, I go abroad tomorrow and buy you a plumb pie'. These were the last words I did hear my sweet child speak, for the pangs of death seized upon her on the Sabbath morning, and so she continued in great agonies (which were very grievous unto us, the beholders) till Tuesday morning, and then my sweet child died at four o'clock in the morning, being the eleventh day of October, and was buried that night.

John, aged 1, 1626
The night before he died he lay crying all that night: 'Mame, Oh John's hand, Oh John's foot.' For he was struck cold all one side of his body, and about three o'clock in the morning Mrs. Trotter that watch with him wakened my wife and I and told us he was departing now. And my wife started up and looked at him. He then being aware of his mother, he said 'Mame, John fall down, op-a-day.' And the next day he had two or three fits . . . and at eleven o'clock at night he said to the maid Jane 'some beer' and she

gave him some beer. Then he said 'op-a-day'. These were the last words that my sweet son John spake, and so ended this miserable life on Tuesday the fifth day of April 1626.

[48], pp. 87–9.

DOCUMENT 3   THE AUTOBIOGRAPHY OF ALICE THORNTON

Mrs Alice Thornton (1626–1707) was a member of a prominent Yorkshire family. She had nine children before her husband's death in 1668, an event on which she reflects here.

That night was spent in somme little slumbers, but very unquiett and full of feares, trimblings, and sad apprehensions. In the morning my brother Denton came home and very disceetely prepared me with good advice and councell to entertaine the Lord's determinate will in all things with patience and submittion, if the worst should fall upon me according to my feares. But withall said that God could raise my dearest joy up againe, were he never soe weake, as I had experience of, if He see it fitt for us, although, indeed, my deare heart was then very weake; at which words my faintings renewed with my exceeding sorrows, for the feares of being deprived of this my sole delight in this world next under God. The Lord pardon my impatience in this conserne, which had for the three last past yeares bin waning him and myselfe from this world, through great and manifold tribulations. Thus, betwixt hopes and fears I remained till the next messenger came, at four o'clock on Thursday, in the affternoone, at which time I receaved newes (for me) of the most tirrable loss that any poor woman could have, in beeing deprived of my sweet and most exceeding dear husband's life.

C. Jackson (ed.), *The Autobiography of Mrs Alice Thornton of East Newton, Co. York*, Surtees Society, 62, 1875, pp. 174–5.

DOCUMENT 4   SELECTIONS FROM THE HOUSEHOLD CENSUS FOR BILSTON, STAFFORDSHIRE, 1695

Houselistings form one of the most important sources for the study of family life in the past. Even a selection from a listing, such as this, gives an impression of the way households were constructed. This example is also unusually interesting because of the comments added about many of those named.

John Hoo, Esq., Widdower.
Mrs. Joan Hoo, Widd. She Dyed Aged & Consumptive December ye 29th, 1703.

Samll. Pipe, Gent. Dyed of a Colick, Nov. 2nd, 1706. Aged abt. 65.
Mrs Howard, his Wife.

Sarah, ⎤ Children of Mr Pipe
Anne,
Dorothy, married to Mr. Davies a Grocer in Chester, Nov. ye 8th, 1701.
Mary, married to Mr. E. Perry, Feb. ye 2nd, 1701. Buried March 18th, 1706
Humphrey, went to Oxford in June as I take itt, 1700. Enter'd in Pembroke Coll.

Tho. Stokes. ⎤
Will. Bayly. } Servts att Mr. Hoo's.
Joanna Horton, ⎦
Will Perry. ⎤
Eliz Perry. } Servts to Mr. Pipe. married to Tho. Stokes of this town.
Eliz Price. ⎦

Eliz. Cooper, Widd.: she was Daughter of Ric. Hammons of Willenhall & was Baptised March ye 27th, 1614, as I found in Wolverhampton Register. She died Jan. 21, 1705/6. Aged 91 yrs.
Ric. Cooper.
Letitia, his Wife.

their children ⎧ Eliz. married to Wm. ye son of Mr. John Turton in Sedgley parish abt. Oct. 16, 1708.
William, married Eliz., ye daughter of ye said Mr. Turton, May ye 1st, 1709.
John.
Richard. he died of a Consumption, March ye 30the, 1701, abt 11 of ye Clock.

Richard Leese, ⎤ who went to Willenhall & married Ric. Molineaux's Daughter.
Ric. Hale, ⎦ Apprentices there (i.e., with the Coopers.)
Jos. Stokes. ⎤
Jane, his Wife. } he and his family went to Dudley, 1701.
Anna, his daughter ⎦
John Smith.
Issac Smith.
Abra'm Smith.
Anne Pinston, servt there: married to Hen. Taylor

Susanna Mousell, Widd.: married to John Bickley.

John ⎤
Catherine ⎥ her children
Elizabeth ⎦ died 8 Apr., 1709, after a long Weakness – ye Kings Evill.

Jos. Perry.
Anne, his Wife.
Joseph. ⎤
Mary. ⎥ Their Children.
William. ⎥
Elizabeth. ⎦
Sarah. ⎤
Sarah Feriday. ⎥ Servants
Mary Beckett. ⎦

John Smith, died 10 May, 1709, Aged, after abt a month's Weakness abt ye middle of ye day [?].
Eliz., his wife, died almost Suddenly of an Apoplexy att Ettingsall, Feb. ye 19, 1709/10
Tho. Smith, Apprentice, died March 20, 1704, of a Feaver.
Thos. Stephens. Married Mary ye Daughter of Wm. Steward.

John Beavan.
Rachel his wife.
John. ⎤
Thomas ⎥ Their Children.
Issac. ⎦
Tho. Hadley. Apprentice.
Edwd. Beavan.
Ric. Norgrove, married Anne Smith.

Thoo. Smith, Senr., died abt 2 or 3 yeares after.
Ann, his wife, died abt an yeare after.
Sarah.
Ann
Sarah Taylor

John Cox.
Eleanor Perry, Widd.
Edward.   ⎤ married Mrs Mary Pepe, Feb. 2, 1701.
          ⎟ their children
Catherine | married to Geo. Perry, Nov. 8, 1701.
Eleanor | married Tho. Ebrall of Balsall, Warwicksh. about end of January,
          ⎦ 1701.

———————

John Perry de Gate.
Mary his wife.
John   ⎤
Alexandra.|
Issabella.| their children
Wiliam. |
Augustine.|
Peter.   ⎦

———————

Thomas, H. R. (ed.), *Bilston Parish Register*, Staffordshire Parish Register Society, privately printed, 1937–38, pp. 178–81.

| DOCUMENT 5 | **EXTRACTS FROM THE BURIAL REGISTER OF ST MICHAEL LE BELFREY, YORK, 1581** |

Parish registers can be used to find a variety of information about family life in the past. This short extract, like many, also contains considerable additional information that can be highly informative about ages at death, and places of baptism.

Johanne Joye, Daughter to Rob'te Joye, christned in the howse at home by ye grace woman, buried the fyft day of april
Mrs. Anne childe, wif to Mr Thomas childe, about xlij yeares of age, was buried the xxijth day of aprill
Randal Loshe, sonne to George Loshe, buried the first day of June, beinge foure months and somewhatt more, oulde
Isabell Jameson, wydowe, aboute thadge of lxviij years, buryed the thirde Day of June
Elizabeth Fale, wif to Edmunde Fale, of xl years of age, buried the xxth day of Julye
Francis Proctour, sonne to Henrie Proctour, beinge baptised at home by the mydwyf, was buried the xxjth Day of Julye

Christofer caverlay, sonne to John caverlay, buryed the xxviijth Day of July, beinge aboute two yeares oulde

John Sargeanson, about xl years of age, buryed the first day of Aug.

John Cowp[er], sonne to John Cowp[er], aboute two years oulde, was buried the vij day of August

Mr Blythe, secretorye and one of the Quenes ma'tyes councellours in these north p'tes, was buryed the xijth day of August

James hudson, sonne to Richard hudson, advocate, was buryed the xiijth day of August, beinge but thre days oulde

Hellen bussye, daughter of John bussye, buried the xxjth of august

Elizabeth Johnson, wydowe, aboute thadge of lx yeares, buryed the xxviijth day of August

Agness Carre, wydowe, about xliiiij^{tie} yeares oulde, buryed the said xxviijth day of August

Anne Bardgement, Daughter of George Bargment, beinge two moneths oulde, was buryed the ixth day of september

Will'm Bowe, about thadge of lvj yeares, buryed the xxth of Sep.

Matthewe walker, sonn to Edwarde walker, beinge vj dayes oulde, buryed the xxixth day of september

Mary Blenkarne, wife of Mr thomas blenkarne, aboute xxxiiij^{tie} yeares oulde, was buryed in the high quyer of St. olyves the thirde day of october

> F. A. Collins (ed.), *The Registers of St. Michael le Belfry, York, Part 1, 1565–1653*, Yorkshire Parish Register Society, 1, 1899, p. 36.

DOCUMENT 6 HEARTH TAX RETURNS, PETER-LE-WILLOWS, THE CITY OF YORK, 1665–74

The Hearth Tax was a graduated assessment based on the number of hearths in a house. These three assessments of part of a parish over a decade demonstrate something of the social structure, how the life cycle affected residence and some of the problems caused by irregular spelling of names.

(a) 1665

Name	Number of Hearths
Henry Belton	1
Thomasson Belton	2
Will. Johnson	1
Will Dobissen	1
Christopher Dinnes	3
Richard Dobinsen	1
Phillep Mennton	2
Rob. Lenne	2

Rich. Mason	2
Will Mennton	1
	16

(b) 1670

Name	Number of Hearths
Mr Henry Bolton	3
Allex Hayward	2
Ann Chapman & Halladay	2
Ann Hornesey	1
Rich. Dobbison	2
Rich Mayson	–
[?] Dynnis	3
John Walton	2
Robt. Allon	2
Willm Dobson	3
Robt Smyth	1
Robt Clarke or Richard Mason	2
William Moncton	1
Mr Charles Blcshre	3
Henry Skelton	1
	29 [28]

(c) 1674

Name	Number of Hearths
Sinolis Spendlore	2
Mr Thomas Bouth	4
Rc. Dobison	2
Wm Dobyson	3
Margt Robins	2
Wm Mountain	1
Robt Clarke	2
Robt Allen	2
Will Mason	1
John Jackson	1
Mr Blashrard	1
	21

York Civic Archives, Hearth Tax M30:22, M30:23 and M30:25.

Extensive use has been made of wills in an attempt to understand both patterns of inheritance and the nature of kinship relationships in the past. This example comes from a gentleman who had no clear heir and therefore reveals rather more detail about his wider relationships and wishes.

In the name of God Amen the thirtieth Day of December in the yeere of our Lord God 1606. I Bray Rolfe of Sarratt in the County of Hartf[or]d gent sicke in body but of p[er]fect minde and memory thanckes be given to Almighty God doe make and ordayne this my last will and Testament in manner and forme followinge. First I bequeath my soule into the handes of Almighty god my maker and my body to be buryed in the p[ar]ish Church of St. Albans soe neere my Fathers corpes as conveniently may be.

Item I give and bequeath to the poore people of St. Albans XXXs to be distributed amongst them at the day of my Buryall. Itm my Will is that my Executors here undernamed shall by their discretions bestowe w[it]hin six monethes after my decease the Soom of £XX of lawfull English money for and towardes the behoofe and benefitt of Ann Ireland al[ia]s Crouche my Kinswomen of Hartf[or]d the same money soe to be placed as that the p[ro]fitt may yeerly redowne to hir and the Heirs of her bodey and that the same stocke or any parte thereof shall not com to the possession or disposition of Edward Crouche hir Husband.

Item I will and bequeath unto Rob[er]t Johnson servant unto my brother James Rolfe six pounds thirteen shillings four pence of lawfull english money to be paid unto him w[i]thin one yeere after my decease. Itm I give and bequeath unto my godson John Rockitt £VI XIIIs IIId. Itm to my Kinsman william Peacocke XXVIs. eight pence to buy him a ringe to wear for my sake. Itm to Dorothy Peacoke XLs. Itm to Samuell Grane and Ann Rockitt XLs a peece all w[hi]ch legacies to be paid w[i]thin one yeere after my decease. Item I give and bequeath unto my kinsman Rob[er]t Gillmett five pounds. Itm to his sonn Henry £V. Itm I give and bequeath to Mary Rolfe daughter of my Brother James £X. Itm to Nicholas Rolfe XLs.

Itm my love and affection to my Sister Ann Kaye and hir sonn Thomas my Will and meaninge is that the howse wherein Thomas Goddriche dwelleth, now morgaged for £L shall not be redeemed by my executors or eyther or them but shall remayne for ever to my said Sister and hir heirs. Itm I doe will and bequeath to Michaell Rolfe sonn of my Brother William deceased if he attaine to the aidge of XXIty yeers the soom of £L of Lawfull English Money to be then paid and deliv[er]ed unto him if he happen to decease before he attaine the said aidge then the foresaid legacy to be of noe effect and I doe bequeath unto Faith Rolfe his sister £XX to be paid at hir day of mariadge or at the aidge of XXIty yeers if she live to be married or attaine the saide aidge and that hir said Brother be livinge. Itm I give and bequeath to Mary Jewett my maide £V of lawfull English money.

Itm my will and meaninge is and I doe require and chardge my Lovinge Brother James Rolfe whom together w[i]th my foresaid Kinsman Robn[er]t Gillmett I make joyntly and wholley my Executors. That if my welbeloved mother dorothy Rolfe doe delive[er] discharge and release my bond w[hi]ch she hath for the enjoyinge of that coppy hold landes or the rentes thereof to my Executoirs that my said Brother his heirs and Ass[igne]s doe enter like bondes quitly to p[er]mitt and suffer my said Mother duringe hir naturall life to feceive p[er]ceive and take of the rent of my Coppy hold Landes the full Soom of £XIII six shillinges she payinge the rentes due to the Lord and not otherwise. And the rest of the rentes I will to be ditayned and kept by my said Brother for the better satisfaction of my debtes & legacies herein bequeatherd. The rest of my goodes Chattells Cattells moveables ymovables & rightes whatsoev[er] I doe appoint my said Executors to take recieve and ymploye towardes the payment of my debtes and legacies. And the remaynder if any be to my said Brother.

In wittnes whereof I have hereunto set my hand and seale the day and yeere first above written.
Bray Rolfe
Sealed subscribed and deliv[er]ed as his last will and Testament to the Executors w[i]thin names in the p[re]sence of John Fryer curate of Sarret
the mark of Thomas Lee
the mark of Alice Jewett
Rob[er]t Johnson no[ta]ry pub[lic].

P. Buller and B. Buller (eds), *Pots, Platters and Ploughs: Sarratt Wills and Inventories 1435–1832*, privately printed, 1992, pp. 80–2.

DOCUMENT 8   ARCHBISHOP PARKER'S *TABLE OF KINDRED AND AFFINITY*, 1563

Parker's table was an attempt to rationalise the legislation on the laws of incest after the chaos left by changes of regime in the middle decades of the century. It was posted in parish churches and prayer books.

A Table of Kindred and Affinity,
Wherein whosoever are related are forbidden in scripture and our laws to marry together.

A man may not marry his:	A woman may not marry her:
1 Grandmother,	1 Grandfather,
2 Grandfather's Wife,	2 Grandmother's Husband,

3	Wife's Grandmother.	3	Husband's Grandfather.
4	Father's Sister,	4	Father's Brother,
5	Mother's Sister,	5	Mother's Brother,
6	Father's Brother's Wife.	6	Father's Sister's Husband.
7	Mother's Brother's Wife,	7	Mother's Sister's Husband,
8	Wife's Father's Sister,	8	Husband's Father's Brother,
9	Wife's Mother's Sister.	9	Husband's Mother's Brother.
10	Mother,	10	Father,
11	Step-Mother,	11	Step-Father,
12	Wife's Mother.	12	Husband's Father.
13	Daughter,	13	Son,
14	Wife's Daughter,	14	Husband's Son,
15	Son's Wife.	15	Daughter's Husband.
16	Sister,	16	Brother,
17	Wife's Sister,	17	Husband's Brother,
18	Brother's Wife.	18	Sister's Husband.
19	Son's Daughter,	19	Son's Son,
20	Daughter's Daughter,	20	Daughter's Son,
21	Son's Son's Wife.	21	Son's Daughter's Husband.
22	Daughter's Son's Wife,	22	Daughter's Daughter's Husband,
23	Wife's Son's Daughter,	23	Husband's Son's Son,
24	Wife's Daughter's Daughter.	24	Husband's Daughter's Son.
25	Brother's Daughter,	25	Brother's Son,
26	Sister's Daughter,	26	Sister's Son,
27	Brother's Son's Wife.	27	Brother's Daughter's Husband.
28	Sister's Son's Wife,	28	Sister's Daughter's Husband,
29	Wife's Brother's Daughter,	29	Husband's Brother's Son,
30	Wife's Sister's Daughter.	30	Husband's Sister's Son.

W. M. Campion and W. J. Beamont (eds), *The Book of Common Prayer*, London, 1871, p. 400.

DOCUMENT 9 *CONSTITUTIONS AND CANONS OF THE CHURCH OF ENGLAND, 1603*

The increasing use of catechisms as a means of instructing and controlling the young can be seen with the inclusion of this duty for ministers in the canons of 1603, which formed the basis of the revised law of the English Church.

59. *Ministers to Catechise every Sunday*
Every Parson, Vicar, or Curate, upon every Sunday and Holy-day, before Evening Prayer, shall, for half an hour or more, examine and instruct the youth and ignorant persons of his parish, in the Ten Commandments, the Articles of

Belief, and in the Lord's Prayer; and shall diligently hear, instruct, and teach them the Catechism set forth in the Book of Common Prayer. And all fathers, mothers, masters and mistresses, shall cause their children, servants, and apprentices, which have not learned the Catechism, to come to the Church at the time appointed, obediently to hear, and to be ordered by the Minister, until they have learned the same. And if any Minister neglect his duty herein, let him be sharply reproved upon the first complaint, and true notice thereof given to the Bishop or Ordinary of the place. If, after submitting himself, he shall willingly offend therein again, let him be suspended; if so the third time, there being little hope that he will be therein reformed, then excommunicated, and so remain until he will be reformed. And likewise if any of the said fathers, mothers, masters, or mistresses, children, servants, or apprentices, shall neglect their duties, as the one sort in not causing them to come, and the other in refusing to learn, as aforesaid; let them be suspended their Ordinaries, (if they be not children,) and if they so persist by the space of a month, then let them be excommunicated.

Anon (ed.), *The Constitutions and Canons Ecclesiastical*, SPCK, London, 1908, p. 34.

DOCUMENT 10   **DEPOSITION BEFORE THE MAYOR AND ALDERMEN OF NORWICH, 1563**

Under the Statute of Artificers of 1563 servants who left their masters without a certificate could be imprisoned and whipped. Here some of the problems of master–servant relations and their consequences are revealed in the attempts of one apprentice to avoid these possibilities.

Robert Myller, of the cittie of Norwich, Tanner, of the age of xvi yeares or ther abowte, examined before Mr William Farrow, Mayor of the Cittie of Norwich, W. Mingay Henry Croke Henry Bacon Jo. Aldrithe, Justices of the peace, on Wednesdaye the xiiiith of Aprrell, Anno 1563, sayth: That he was in the servyce with one William George of Hempton, Tannor, and dwelte with hym by the space of Thre yeares, And upon a tyme aboute sevenight before candlemas Last paste the wyfe of the sayde William George ded falloute with this examinate and Rebuked hym for his worke very moche, And this examinate sayed unto hys dame: I am sory that I cannot please you, but yf my Sarvice maynot please you, yf you and my Master Will geve me Leave to departe I shall provide me of a service in some place I truste. And heruppon his sayde dame declaryd un to her husbonde the same night that the sayde Robart Myller coulde be content to go from hym and to place hym selfe in some other survice. And therupon he callyd this examinate unto hym and askyd hym whether he wolde go from hym or not, and he sayde: for that my survice cannot please you nor my dame If you will geve me Leve to departe I canbe contentyd to departe, and then the sayde William George his Master sayde: with a good will you shall departe and provide yourselfe of a Master so well as you can. And there upon he drewe to his purse and payed to this examinate seven shillings in mony that he ought hym for certeyne calve skynnys that he had solde of his. And on the Sundaye mornyng this examinate came to his sayde Master to take his leve, And then his sayde Master sayde unto him seying: you will go a waye, you shall not go owte of the hunderde, but you shall serve eyther Mr Clyfton or ells Mr Raymer in husbondry. And this deponent sayed: Master, I have served thes thre yeares in your occupacion and can no skyll in husbandry and I wilbe lothe to lose all this tyme that I have served in the occupacon. And then the sayed William George sayde: Tarry tyll Sondaye and you shall have a new payer of shoos; and so this examinate tarryed styll ther with the sayde William George tyll the Tewesdaye next followyng, and in that tyme he had understandyng that ther was a warrant procured for hym to serve in husbondry, and thereupon he cam from his sayde Master thesayde Tewesday, And so cam strayght to Norwich and placed hym selfe in the service of one Richarde Smethe, Tanner. And further this examinate saythe that the sayde Richarde Smythe sent hym from Norwiche to Elmeham Fayer on our laydys daye with certeyne lether to sell, And there the sayde William George met with this examinate and sayde unto hym: How sayest thou Robyn? hadest not thou as good to have [?] served me for thre yeares as to serve where thou doest serve for vii yeares? for now thou arte bounde thou cannest not get owte of the Cittie nowe [?] . . .

R. H. Tawney, and E. Power (eds), *Tudor Economic Documents*, vol. 1, Longmans, London, 1924, pp. 350–1.

DOCUMENT 11   **THE DIARY OF RALPH JOSSELIN, ON HIS YOUTH AND COURTSHIP, 1639–40**

Josselin (1617–83) was a clergyman in Earls Colne, Essex for most of his life. He has left us one of the fullest and most revealing diaries from the early modern period. Here, at the opening of his book, he describes his youth and courtship.

. . . the Lords day being [Octob:] 6: was my eye fixed with love upon a Mayde; and hers upon mee: who afterwards proved my wy wife: Decemb: 13: my uncle Mr Joslin in Norfolke, sent mee the offer of a place [by] him; but my affection to that mayde that god had layd out to be my wife would not suffer mee to stirre, so I gave the messenger 5^s. and sent him away. in that month of December I was ordayned Deacon by the Bishop of Peterburg. the charges amounted to: I^{li}. 14^s. 9. in my jorn[ey]. in my returne I preached at Deane. December 25^t. and coming home from hence, I read prayers at Olny, and that day found Jane Consrable the mayde before mentioned in our house. which was the beginning of our acquaintance. the next Lords day I preached at Olny: on Acts. 16:31. [and] so also on. Jan: 1: Newyears day: at night invited to supper to Goodman Gaynes: I went in to call Goodwife shepheard, and their my Jane being I stayed with her, which was our first proposall of the match one to another, which wrought a mutual promise one to another on: 23: and by all out consents a Contract: Sept. 28. 1640: and our marriage. October. 28. following . . .

[9], pp. 7–8.

DOCUMENT 12   DEPOSITION OF BRIDGET PAKEMAN IN A DEFORMATION SUIT BEFORE THE ESSEX ARCHDEACON'S COURT, 1570

The records of the church courts throw interesting light on the problems associated with sexuality. This case of what we would now call sexual harassment, shows the vulnerability of serving girls and the importance of reputation, even for men.

She dwelt some time at Wrabness, first with one Godfrey and after with Mr. [Thomas] Sayer, parson there, three quarters of a year, during the which time Sayer would have ravished her, first flattering her and embracing her when she was turning a flooring of malt and promised her if his wife died of child he would marry her and attempted to handle her shamefully, taking up her clothes. Another time on the kell [kiln] as she was heaving of malt, at which time using her as before she fell out with him and was going away from him but he coming after her stayed her. And another time about midsummer she having gathered a bundle of rushes and gathering up the old rushes to have stowed the hall, Sayer came to her, his hose being down, and did shamefully use her, at which time she was forced to take him by the members to save herself, wherewith Sayer gave her a blow on the ear and therewithal departed. Howbeit she denieth that he had his pleasure of her at the time.

[4], p. 212.

DOCUMENT 13   THE COURT ROLLS OF ACOMB, YORK, 1575

Manorial rolls represent the function of the English legal system on almost its lowest level. Most of the work of these courts was concerned with agricultural matters, even if we exclude the transfer of land, which was their primary function. However, these extracts throw some light on family relations and the nature of concerns about gender and age in the period.

1577
Presentments

Wm. Vesse for an affray against John Vesse, his son	3s.	4d.
John Vesse for drawing blood of Wm. Vesse, his father	6s.	8d.

. . .

Penalties

Edward Smythe, John Vesse, Thos. Wood, Wm. Nabelsone and Wm. Monkton not to allow their wives to chide or scold with their neighbours each	3s.	4d.
Elizabeth Blanke not to chide or scold with her neighbours and to kepe hir house in the night season and not be an esinge droper under mens' windows	5s.	0d.

. . .

1580
Presentments

Hy. Rundall and Ric. Butterfeilde, servants of Simon Butterfeilde, for making an affray on Stephen Skadlocke	3s.	4d.

. . .

Thos. Smythe, brewer, for allowing other men's children and servants to eat hens in his house in the night time	4d.

H. Richardson (ed.), *The Court Rolls of the Manor of Acomb, 1*, Yorkshire Archaeological Society Record Series, 131, 1969, pp. 60–9.

DOCUMENT 14   **PAPER IN THE MICHAELMASS SESSIONS ROLL, ESSEX ARCHDEACON'S COURT, 1583**

Popular sanctions against perceived breaches of sexual mores are highly revealing of popular attitudes to sexuality. The following verse was probably pinned up on a door beside cuckold's horns and formed part of the evidence in a defamation suit.

Here dwelleth an arrant bichant whore,
Such one as deserves the cart.
Her name is Margaret Townsend now.
The horn showns her desert.
Fie, of honesty, fie, fie,
Your whore's head is full of jealousy.
Therefore I pray your whore's tricks fly,
And learn to live more honestly.
Alack for woe. Why should I do so?
It will cause a sorrowful hey-ho.

Thus do I end my simple verse,
He that meeteth her husband, a horned beast.

[3], p. 68.

Thomas Becon (c. 1512–c. 1567) was chaplain to Archbishop Cranmer and Protector Somerset. He was a radical Protestant who urged further reform, publishing a number of polemical works, particularly directed against Catholicism. David's Harp *was a exposition based on Psalm 115.*

Let husbands love their wives as their own bodies, and be not bitter, churlish or unkind to them, but 'give honour unto them as unto the weaker vessels, and as unto them that are fellow-heirs with them of the grace of life'.

Likewise let the 'wives be in subjection to their husbands, as unto the Lord' in all things, and so behave themselves as it becometh women of an honest and godly conversation. 'Let them array themselves in comely apparel with shamefacedness and discreet behaviour; not with braided hair, or gold, or pearl, or costly array, but with such as becometh women that profess godliness though good work'. Let the 'inward man of the heart be uncorrupt, with a meek and quiet spirit, which before God is much set by. For this manner in the old time did the holy women which trusted in God [en]tire themselves, and were obedient to their husbands; even as Sara obeyed Abraham, and called him lord, whose daughter the wives are, so long as they do well, not being afraid for any trouble'.

Let 'fathers not rate their children, lest they be of a desperate mind, but bring them up in the nurture and information of the Lord.'

Let the 'children also obey their parents in all things; for that is well pleasing unto the Lord.'

Let 'masters do unto their servants that which is just and equal, putting away threatenings, and know that they also have a master in heaven, with whom there is no respect of persons'.

Let the 'servants again be obedient unto their bodily masters in all things, with fear and trembling, in singleness of heart, as unto Christ; not with service only in the eyesight, as men-pleasers; but as the servants of Christ; doing the will of God from the heart, with good will. Let them think that they serve the Lord and not men, and let them be sure, that whatsoever good a man doeth, he shall receive it again of the Lord, whether he be bond or free.'

To conclude, let every one of us do our duty, and live according to the vocation whereunto God hath called us. So shall it come to pass, that we shall not walk unworthy the kindness of God. So shall we truly pay our vows unto the Lord. So shall we faithfully perform that which we heretofore promised in baptism. So shall we daily more and more increase in the love of God, and taste more plenteously of his bounteous gifts.

J. Ayre (ed.), *The Early Works of Thomas Becon*, Parker Society, Cambridge, 1843, p. 287.

DOCUMENT 16 RICHARD BAXTER, *THE POOR MAN'S FAMILY BOOK*, 1674

Baxter (1615–91) was a minister of the Church of England, but his Puritan leanings led to his exclusion from the Church after 1662 and eventual imprisonment. He published several works, including this attempt to reproduce views on family life for a relatively humble audience.

The Special Duties of the Husband
They are: 1. To exercise love and authority together (never separated) to his wife. 2. To be the chief teacher and governor of the family and the provider for its maintenance. 3. To excel the wife in knowledge and patience, and to be her teacher and guide in the matters of God, and to be the chief in bearing infirmities and trials. 4. To keep up the wife's authority and honour in the family over inferiors.

The Special Duties of the Wives
1. To excel in love. 2. To be obedient to their husbands and examples therein to the rest of the family. 3. Submissively to learn of their husbands (that can teach them) and not to be self-conceited, teaching, talkative or imperious. 4. To subdue their passions, deny their own fancies and wills, and not to tempt their husbands to satisfy their humours and vain desires in pride, excess, revenge or any evil, not to rob God and the poor by a proud and wasteful humour (as the wives of gentlemen ordinarily do). 5. To govern their tongues, that their words may be few and sober; and to abhor a running and scolding tongue. 6. To be contented in every condition, and not to torment their husbands and themselves with impatient murmurings. 7. To avoid the childish vanity of gaudy apparel, and following vain fashions of the prouder sort. And to abhor their vice that waste precious time in curious and tedious dressings, gossipings, visits and feasts. 8. To help on the maintenance of the family by frugality and by their proper care and labour. 9. Not to dispose of their husband's estate without his consent, either explicit or implicit. Above all, to be constant helpers of the holy education of their children. . . . And so they may become chief instruments of the reformation and welfare of churches and kingdoms of the world.

R. Baxter, *The Poor Man's Family Book*, London, 1674.

Richard Gough, a farmer on the verge of being a gentleman, left us one of the most remarkable documents of the period, a history of all the families in the parish of Myddle in Shropshire, organised by the pews they occupied in the parish church. It provides countless insights into family life, and social life in general, in the early modern period.

The second peiw on the North side of the North Isle

This seat belongs whoally to the farme called the Hollins, whose leawan is 1s. 6d. This farme is the Earle of Bridgewater's land; and it is reported that the house was a dayry house belonging to Myddle Castle. I can give no accompt of any tenant of this farme, further than Humphrey Reynolds who was Churchwarden of this parish when the register was transcribed in Mr. Wilton's time. One William Cleaton married a daughter of this Reynolds, and soe beecame tenant of this farme, and had a lease for the lives of himselfe, his wife, and Francis, his eldest son. Hee lived in good repute, and served several offices in this parish. Hee had 4 sons. I. Francis, who displeased his father in marrying with Margaret Vaughan, a Welsh woman, sometimes servant to Mr. Kinsaton, Rector of Myddle, and therefore hee gave him lytle or nothing dureing his life. 2. Issac who married a daughter of one White, of Meriton, and had a good portion with her. The widow Lloyd, of Leaton, who is very rich in land and money, is a daughter of this Issac. 3. Samuell, who married Susan, the daughter of Thomas Jukes, of Newton on the Hill, and lived a tenant to Mr. Hunt, in Basechurch. 4. Richard, an untowardly person. He married Annie, the daughter of William Tyller, a woman as infamous as him-selfe. 'Pares cum paribus facilime congregantur' [Like is most often brought together with like]. The parents on both sides were displeased, (or seemed soe,) with this match, and therefore allowed the new marryed couple noe maintenance. Richard Cleaton soone out run his wife, and left his wife bigge with child. Shee had a daughter, which was brought up by Allen Challoner, (the smith) of Myddle; for his wife was related to William Tyler. This daugh-ter came to bee a comely and handsome woman. Shee went to live in service toards Berrinton, beyond Shrewsbury, but I have not heard of her lately.

   Richard Cleaton went into the further part of this Country; and below Bridgenorth hee gott another wife, and had several children by her. At last, Anne Tyler, his first wife, caused him to bee apprehended, and indicted him att an Assizes at Bridgenorth upon the statute of Poligami. Shee proved that shee was marryied to him, but could not prove that he was married to the other woman, but only that he lived with her, and had children by her. The other woman denied that shee was marryed to him; and thereupon the Judge sayd 'Then thou art a whore.' To which shee answered 'the worse luck mine my lord.' Cleaton was acquitted, and went out of the country [ie the county] with the other woman, and I never heard more of him.

[5], pp. 92–3.

DOCUMENT 18 NICHOLAS CULPEPER, *A DIRECTORY FOR MIDWIVES*, 1651

Culpeper (1616–54) was a Cambridge-educated physician and astrologer. His works on medicine were widely read among interested parties. These extracts give an indication of the limits of even professional knowledge about women's physiology and the nature of childbirth.

Medicines for a woman that would have children
By way of a caution:
1. Use not the act of copulation too often: some say it makes the womb slippery, I rather think it makes the womb more willing to open than shut. Saitety gluts the womb and makes it unfit to do its office, and that's the reason whores so seldom have children; and also the reason why women after long absence of their husbands, when they come again usually soon conceive.
2. Let the time be convenient, for fear of surprise hinders conception.
3. Let it be after perfect digestion; let neither hunger nor drunkeness be upon the man or woman.
4. Let the desire of copulation come naturally, and not by provocation. The greater the woman's desire for copulation is, the more subject is she to conceive.
5. Women are most subject to conceive a day or two after their monthly terms are stayed.
6. Avoid eating or bearing about you all such things as cause barreness: such be the none of a stag's heart, emeralds, sapphires, ivy berries, jet, burnet, leaves and roots, hart's tongue, steel dust, mints &c.
7. Apish ways and manners of copulation hinder conception.

[1], p. 124.

DOCUMENT 19 *A CAVEAT FOR YOUNG MEN, OR THE BAD HUSBAND TURN'D THIRSTY*

Popular ballads provide a fascinating, if sometimes confusing, insight into popular expectations and ideas about some aspects of family life. This extract from a mid-seventeenth-century ballad is typical in its moral tone, but unusually highlights the expectations on husbands by concentrating on the evils of drink.

This Caveat may serve both for Old and yong,
For to remember that Old Age will come;

If you these Verses do minde and read,
I hope hereafter you will take better heeed:
This Song it was set forth and penn'd
To teach Bad Husbands to amend,
Therefore bad husbands mend your lives,
And be more kinder to your Wives.

To the Tune of, Hey ho my Honey.

All you young Ranting Blades,
that spend your time in vain,
Remember that old age,
you cannot it refrain:
And whilst that you are young,
this Caveat take of me,
Be ruled by no tempting tongue,
to bring you to poverty.
I have been a bad husband long
and have spent store of silver and gold,
Yet now Ile save something whist I am yong,
to keep me when I am old.

I had good store of means,
and I liv'd most gallantly:
But yet upon Whores and Queans,
I spent it by and by:
My Hoastis she was full of laughter,
so long as I had money good store;
And my Children must drink butt water,
whilst I in the Ale-house did roar.
I have been &c.

My Wife would me intreat,
the Alehouse to refrain;
Then I with anger great,
made answear straight again:
If you begin to scold,
then I will hang thy coat;
What woman her tongue can hold,
when a man swallows all down his throat.
I have been, &c. . . .

W. G. Day (ed.), *The Pepys Ballads*, vol. 2, Brewer,
Cambridge, 1987, p. 22.

GERVASE HOLLES, MEMORIALS OF THE HOLLES FAMILY, 1656

Gervase Holles (1607–75) was a Royalist in exile in the Netherlands when he put together this account of the history of his family. This extract describes the last years of his grandfather, also called Gervase Holles, and highlights some of the problems of old age among the gentry.

. . . (being now very olde) he left London and retired himselfe into the country desirous to end his dayes amongst his children and kindred. So having shipt his trunckes and household stuffe he went to sea himselfe and sayled from Gravesend to Hull about the end of February, a strange voyage and in a strange season for his yeares, being then about 74 yeares of age. From thence he came to Grimesby to my father wth whom he continued about a yeare untill Sr Percivall Willughby, by insinuating letters and praetence of better ayre, enticed him to him at Wollaton, where he continued about fower yeares: untill at length falling dangerously sicke Sr Percivall most dishonestly and ungratefully, in the extremity of his weaknes, employes one Percival Hynde a parson and one Harvy his servant to guide my grandfather's hand to a release of all the debtes he owed him and after y^t set his seale to themselves. But upon his recovery, he, getting notice of what was done, bid farewell to Sr Percivall Willughby and returned backe to my father . . .

He lived after he made his last will just two yeares and two days and died at Great Grimesby in the law wainscot roome of my house there upon the fifth day of March 1627. He continued sick but two dayes nor could I understand (I was then in London) y^t he died of any disease save the incurable one of olde age. Had he lived until May day following he had accomplisht 81 yeares. His close was pious and his exit so free from sense of payne that he seemed to steale away out of the world, and he retayned his memory to the last.

A. C. Wood, (ed.), *Memorials of the Holles Family 1493–1656 by Gervase Holles,*
Camden Society, 3rd series, 55, 1937, pp. 122–4.

MEMORIAL BRASS TO SIR RICHARD FITZLEWES AND HIS WIVES FROM INGRAVE, ESSEX, 1528

Memorials to the dead provide insights, not only into ideas and emotions regarding death, but also of family life in general. The two examples below illustrate some of the major changes that occurred in this form of commemoration in the early modern period.

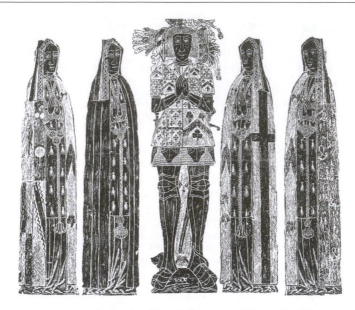

M. Clayton, *Catalogue of Rubbings of Brasses and Incised Slabs*, HM Stationery
Office, London, 1915.

**DOCUMENT 22   MEMORIAL BRASS TO THOMAS CAREW AND
HIS WIFE FROM HACCOMBE, DEVON, 1656**

M. Clayton, *Catalogue of Rubbings of Brasses and Incised Slabs*, HM Stationery Office,
London, 1915.

DOCUMENT 23   JOHN LOCKE, *SOME THOUGHTS CONCERNING EDUCATION*, 1693

Locke (1632–1704) was a philosopher, physician, scientist and politician. He is best remembered for his political ideas, but he also made a major contribution to the debate on the nature of the family. Here he outlines his view of the discipline of children, on which his Enlightenment successors were to build and which already owed much to Humanist and Protestant thinkers.

If severity carried to the highest pitch does prevail, and works a cure upon the present unruly distemper, it is often bringing in the room of it worse and more dangerous disease, by breaking the mind; and then, in the place of a disorderly young fellow, you have a low-spirited moped creature: who, however, with his un-natural sobriety he may please silly people, who commend tame inactive children, because they make no noise, nor give them any trouble; yet, at last, will probably prove as uncomfortable a thing to his friends, as he will be, all his life, an useless thing to himself and others.

Beating then, and all other sorts of slavish and corporal punishments, are not the discipline fit to be used in the education of those who would have wise, good, and ingenious men; and therefore very rarely to be applied, and that only on great occasions, and in cases of extremity. On the other side, to flatter children by rewards of things that are pleasant to them, is as carefully to be avoided. He that will give to his apples, or sugar-plums, or what else of this kind he is more delighted with, to make him learn his book, does but authorise his love of pleasure, and cocker up that dangerous propensity, which he ought by all means to subdue and stifle in him.

P. Gay (ed.), *John Locke on Education*, Columbia University Press, New York, 1964, pp. 34–5.

DOCUMENT 24   MARY ROBINSON, *A LETTER TO THE WOMEN OF ENGLAND, ON THE INJUSTICE OF MENTAL SUBORDINATION*, 1799

Mary Robinson (1758–1800) was a poet, novelist, actress and mistress of the Prince of Wales. Writing here at the end of her life under the name of Anne Francis Randall, her views contrast sharply with the conduct books of the preceding centuries.

If a women be the weaker creature, why is she employed in laborious avocations? why compelled to endure the fatigue of household drudgery; to scrub, to scower, to labour, both late and early while the powdered lacquery only waits at the chair, or behind the carriage of his employer? Why are the women, in many parts of the kingdom, permitted to follow the plough; to perform the laborious business of the dairy; to work in our manufactories; to wash, to brew, and to bake, while men are employed in measuring lace and ribands; folding gauzes; composing artificial bouquets; fancying feathers, and mixing cosmetics for the preservation of beauty? I have seen, and every inhabitant of the metropolis may, during the summer season, behold strong Welsh girls carrying on their heads strawberries, and other fruits from the vicinity of London to Covent-Garden market, in heavy loads which they repeat three, four, and five times daily, for a very small pittance; while the *male* domesticks of our nobility are revelling in luxury, to which even their lords are strangers. Are thus women compelled to labour, because they are of the WEAKER SEX?

V. Jones (ed.), *Women in the Eighteenth Century*, Routledge, London, 1990, p. 238.

DOCUMENT 25   **A LETTER TO THE MASTER OF THE ROLLS, FROM THE PRIVY COUNCIL, 1590**

The problems of both proto-industrialisation and urbanisation were no more keenly felt than in the City of London, which endured a radical increase in its size across our period. The problems this created for family life, and the fears of central government, can be seen in the attempts to force local authorities to deal with the problem in the sixteenth century.

Wheras yt pleased the Queen's Majestie more than two yeres past to command proclamacion to be published for the restrayning and prohibiting of new building of howses and tenements for habitacion in and about the Citie of London, whereby as by the access of multitudes of people to inhabit the same and the pestering of many families in one smale house or tenemente termed inmats and undersitters, the Cittie hath ben over largelie increased to the decaie of other townes, bouroughes and villages within the Realme, but also th'infeccion of the plague thereby the rather continued and augmented to the los of great nombers of people, the inconveniencie whereof as of other like disorders hereby followed and like further to ensue (which at large were expressed in the said proclamacion) having been then by her Majestie and us graciouslie and gravely considered, moved her to take ordre for the reforming thereof and gave auctoritie to you as wel to forbid and inhibit al such buildinges as to punish the persons that after the publishing of the said proclamacion should attempt to build and erect houses and tenementes contrarie to her Majestie's prohibicion therein contained. Howbeit her Majestie's gracious intent and care had from [sic] the preventing of th'inconviencies and disorders aforesaid have taken so slendre effect as sithence the said proclamacion published the building of houses and tenementes about the Citie hath contin[u]ed and gretlie increased, which her Majestie conceaveth to have grown especiallie by the necligence and remisnes of you to whom the charge and trust thereof hath bin comitted, whereat her Highness and we do not a litle marvaile. Her pleasure and straight comaundment therefore is that with all diligence upon the receipt hereof you call unto you some of the Justices of Peace in the countie of Middlesex or any that is a Lord of any liberties, or steuards or bailives, and imparting unto them the tenour of theis our lettres, you proceed by waie of inquisition upon the oaths of good and sufficient persons, and to discover and find out throw all parties of your jurisdiction what houses &c. have ben from the tyme of the prohibicion mentioned in the proclamacion until this daie to the same builded and errected by any person or persons, and who hath bin the principle offend-ours therein, and thereof receiving their presentements by oath, to make a formal certificat thereof in writing to be sent to us with al expedicion, and to take good bonds of such as shalbe found to have so offended to appeare before us at Star Chamber to answer their offence according to the tenour of her Majestie's proclamacion at such daie and tyme as shalbe signified unto you . . .

R. H. Tawney and E. Power (eds), *Tudor Economic Documents*, 1, Longmans, London, 1924, pp. 130–1.

DOCUMENT 26   DANIEL DEFOE, *A TOUR THROUGH THE WHOLE ISLAND OF GREAT BRITAIN*, 1726

Defoe's (1660–1731) impressionistic account of his tours of Britain contains one of the best descriptions of the functioning of proto-industrial cloth manu-facturing in West Yorkshire and the villages around Halifax and Huddersfield.

Among the manufacturers houses are likewise scattered an infinite number of cottages or small dwellings, in which dwell the workmen which are employed, the women and children of whom, are always busy carding, spinning, &c. so that no hands being unemploy'd, all can gain their bread, even from the youngest to the antient; hardly any thing above four years old, but its hands are sufficient to it itself.

This is the reason also why we saw so few people without doors; but if we knock'd at the door of any of the master manufacturers, we presently saw a house full of lusty fellows, some at the dye-fat, some dressing the cloths, some in the loom, some one thing, some another, all hard at work and full employed upon the manufacture, and all seeming to have sufficient business.

G. D. H. Cole, and D. C. Browning (eds), *Daniel Defoe, A Tour Through the Whole Island of Great Britain*, vol. 2, Everyman, London, 1962, p. 195.

GLOSSARY

Affinity   Kinship which copies consanguinity. Affinal kin are those where a relationship is created by law or custom.

Aggregative analysis   The production of statistics concerned with demography by comparing different pieces of quantitative evidence.

Bi-lateral descent   A system of kinship where descent is counted through both mothers and fathers, as in Western Europe since the early medieval period.

Conjugal couple   A man and women, who are (usually) married.

Conjugal family   One of many terms to describe families composed only of parents and their children, but lacking implications of mental or residential isolation that are associated with the term 'nuclear family'.

Consanguinity   Kinship through 'blood'. The most obvious type of kinship relationship in which kin share a biological relationship.

Dispensation   Permission to disregard some of the laws of the Church, most obviously those on marriage. Henry VIII had a dispensation from the pope to marry Catherine of Aragon, the wife of his dead brother, and his case for divorce argued that the pope had no right to grant such an exception to God's law. Dispensations were discontinued in the Church of England from 1540.

Ego-centred kinship   A kinship system based on individuals where each has a distinct set of kin and distinct names for them. Sometimes also known as an Eskimo system. This is the pattern that has been predominant in Western Europe since the early middle ages.

Elementary family   Another term for parents and their children.

Family of orientation   The family into which an individual is born and where they are usually brought up.

Family of procreation   The family that an individual creates, usually for the purpose of having children.

Family reconstitution   A method of deriving findings from demographic evidence by connecting the pieces of evidence concerning individual and family groups.

Mean Household Size   A measure of the average numbers of persons resident within a household in a given community.

Mores   The social rules and expectations of a society.

Nuclear family   One of many terms to describe families composed only of parents and their children. The implication is usually one of mental or residential isolation.

Patriarchal family   A family form identified by Frederick Le Play in which relatively distant kin share residence and/or ownership of property.

Patriarchy Rule by fathers, and therefore by old men. It is often used to describe a system where women are subordinate to men.

Primogeniture A system of inheritance where the eldest son acquires the entire estate on the death of his father.

Spiritual kinship The most common term for relationships that mirror consanguinity, but are usually created through religious ceremonies. The most important in medieval and early modern England was godparenthood.

Spousals A promise of marriage in the present tense in front of witnesses, or, if in the future tense, if followed by the sexual act. These were binding in popular opinion and law as much as marriage.

Stem family (famille souche) A family form identified by Frederick Le Play, in which one child (usually the eldest or youngest son) remains in the parental home, even when married, and then inherits the estate on his parent's death.

Strict settlement A system which helped to keep the estate of a man without sons intact by entailing it away from daughters towards a single male relative.

Unigeniture A system of inheritance where an estate is divided equally between children on the death of their parents. Sometimes only sons inherit, but sometimes all children.

Unstable family The term used by Frederick Le Play to describe families composed only of the conjugal couple and their children.

BIBLIOGRAPHY

USEFUL COLLECTIONS OF PRIMARY SOURCES

1 Aughterson, K. (ed.), *Renaissance Women, Constructions of Femininity in England*, Routledge, London, 1995.

2 Davis, N. (ed.), *The Paston Letters: A Selection in Modern Spelling*, Oxford University Press, Oxford, 1983.

3 Emmison, F. G. (ed.), *Elizabethan Life: Disorder*, Essex County Council, Chelmsford, 1970.

4 Emmison, F. G. (ed.), *Elizabethan Life: Morals and the Church Courts*, Essex County Council, Chelmsford, 1973.

5 Gough, R., *The History of Myddle*, (ed.) Hey, D., Penguin, London, 1981.

6 Houlbrooke, R. A. (ed.), *English Family Life 1576–1716: An Anthology from Diaries*, Blackwells, Oxford, 1988.

7 Kirby, J. (ed.), *The Plumpton Letters and Papers*, Camden Society, fifth series, 8, 1996.

8 MacCulloch, D., and Hughes, P. (eds), 'A bailiff's list and chronicle from Worcester', *Antiquaries Journal*, 75, 1995.

9 Macfarlane, A. (ed.), *The Diary of Ralph Josselin 1616–83*, Oxford University Press, Oxford, 1976.

10 Moody, J., (ed.), *The Private Life of an Elizabethan Lady: the Diary of Lady Margaret Hoby, 1599–1605*, Sutton, Stroud, 1998.

11 Opie, P., and Opie, I. (eds), *The Oxford Dictionary of Nursery Rhymes*, Oxford University Press, Oxford, 1951.

12 Parkinson, R. (ed.), *The Autobiography of Henry Newcome*, 2 vols, Chetham Society, old series, 26 and 27, 1852.

USEFUL GENERAL SOCIAL AND RELIGIOUS HISTORIES

13 Collinson, P., *The Birthpangs of Protestant England: Religious and Cultural Change in the Sixteenth and Seventeenth Centuries*, Macmillan, Basingstoke, 1988.

14 Coward, B., *Social Change and Continuity in Early Modern England 1590–1750*, Longman, London, 1988.

15 Daunton, M. J., *Progress and Poverty: An Economic and Social History of Britain 1700–1850*, Oxford University Press, Oxford, 1995.

16 Duffy, E., *The Stripping of the Altars: Traditional Religion in England 1400–1580*, Yale University Press, New Haven, CT, 1992.

17 French, K., Gibbs, G., and Kümin, B. (eds), *The Parish in English Life 1400–1600*, Manchester University Press, Manchester, 1997.

18   Laslett, P., *The World We Have Lost – Further Explored*, Methuen, London, 1965, 1983.
19   Malcolmson, R. W., *Life and Labour in England 1700–1780*, Hutchinson, London, 1981.
20   Sharpe, J. A., *Crime in Early Modern England, 1550–1750*, Longman, London, 1984.
21   Sharpe, J. A., *Early Modern England: A Social History*, Arnold, London, 1987.
22   Spufford, M., *Small Books and Pleasant Histories: Popular Fiction and its Readership in Seventeenth-century England*, Cambridge University Press, Cambridge, 1981.
23   Wrightson, K., *English Society 1580–1680*, Hutchinson, London, 1982.

GENERAL HISTORIES AND HISTORIOGRAPHIES OF THE FAMILY

24   Abbott, M., *Family Ties, English Families 1540–1920*, Routledge, London, 1993.
25   Anderson, M., *Approaches to the History of the Western Family 1500–1914*, Cambridge University Press, Cambridge, 1980, 1995.
26   Casey, J., *The History of the Family*, Blackwells, Oxford, 1989.
27   Durston, C., *The Family in the English Revolution*, Blackwells, Oxford, 1989.
28   Flandrin, J. L., *Families in Former Times: Kinship, Household and Sexuality*, Cambridge University Press, Cambridge, 1979.
29   Goody, J., *The Development of the Family and Marriage in Europe*, Cambridge University Press, Cambridge, 1983.
30   Goody, J., *The European Family*, Blackwells, Oxford, 2000.
31   Gottlieb, B., *The Family in the Western World*, Oxford University Press, Oxford, 1993.
32   Hanawalt, B. A., *The Ties That Bound: Peasant Families in Medieval England*, Oxford University Press, Oxford, 1986.
33   Houlbrooke, R. A., *The English Family 1450–1700*, Longman, London, 1984.
34   Laslett, P., *Family Life and Illicit Love in Earlier Generations: Essays in Historical Sociology*, Cambridge University Press, Cambridge, 1977.
35   Mitteraur, M., and Sieder, R., *The European Family*, Blackwells, Oxford, 1972.

IMPORTANT LOCAL STUDIES

36   Chalklin, C. W., *Seventeenth-century Kent: A Social and Economic History*, Longman, London, 1965.
37   Fletcher, A., *A County Community at Peace and War: Sussex 1600–1660*, Longman, London, 1975.
38   Hey, D. G., *An English Rural Community: Myddle under the Tudors and Stuarts*, Leicester University Press, Leicester, 1974.
39   James, M. E., *Family, Lineage and Civil Society: A Study of the Politics and Mentality in the Durham Region 1500–1640*, Clarendon Press, Oxford, 1974.
40   Levine, D., and Wrightson, K., *The Making of an Industrial Society: Whickham 1560–1765*, Oxford University Press, Oxford, 1991.

41   Phythian-Adams, C., *Desolation of a City: Coventry and the Urban Crisis of the Late Middle Ages*, Cambridge University Press, Cambridge, 1979.

42   Razi, Z., *Life, Marriage and Death in a Medieval Parish: Economy, Society and Demography in Halesowen 1270–1400*, Cambridge University Press, Cambridge, 1981.

43   Spence, R. T., 'The pacification of the Cumberland Borders, 1593–1628', *Northern History*, 13, 1977.

44   Spufford, M., *Contrasting Communities: English Villagers in the Sixteenth and Seventeenth Centuries*, Sutton, London, 1974, 2000.

45   Watts, S. J., and Watts, S. J., *From Border to Middle Shire: Northumberland 1586–1625*, Leicester University Press, Leicester, 1975.

46   Wrightson, K., and Levine, D., *Poverty and Piety in an English Village: Terling 1525–1700*, Oxford University Press, Oxford, 1979, 1995.

STUDIES OF INDIVIDUAL FAMILIES

47   Macfarlane, A., *The Family Life of Ralph Josselin, a Seventeenth-century Clergyman: An Essay in Historical Anthropology*, Cambridge University Press, Cambridge, 1970.

48   Seaver, P. S., *Wallington's World: A Puritan Artisan in Seventeenth-century London*, Methuen, London, 1985.

49   Verney, H., *The Verneys of Claydon: A Seventeenth-century English Family*, Pergamon Press, London, 1968.

50   Winchester, B., *Tudor Family Portrait*, Jonathan Cape, London, 1955.

STUDIES OF EMOTIONS AND FAMILY LIFE

51   de Mause, L. (ed.), *The History of Childhood*, Souvenir Press, London, 1976.

52   Mount, F., *The Subversive Family: An Alternative History of Love and Marriage*, Jonathan Cape, London, 1982.

53   O'Day, R., *Family and Family Relationships 1500–1900: England, France and the United States of America 1500–1900*, Macmillan, Basingstoke, 1994.

54   Shorter, E., *The Making of the Modern Family*, Collins, London, 1976.

55   Stone, L., *Family, Sex and Marriage in England 1500–1800*, Weidenfeld and Nicholson, London, 1977.

56   Trumbach, R., *The Rise of the Egalitarian Family: Aristocratic Kinship and Domestic Relations in Eighteenth-century England*, Academic Press, New York, 1978.

HOUSEHOLD STUDIES

57   Goose, N., 'Household size and structures in early-Stuart Cambridge', in Barry, J. (ed.), *The Tudor and Stuart Town: A Reader in Urban History 1530–1688*, Longman, London, 1990.

58   Laslett, P., and Wall, R. (eds), *Household and Family in Past Time: Comparative Studies in the Size and Structure of the Domestic Group over the Last Three*

Centuries in England, France, Serbia, Japan and Colonial North America, with Further Materials from Western Europe, Cambridge University Press, Cambridge, 1972.

59 Tadmor, N., 'The concept of the household-family in eighteenth-century England', *Past and Present*, 151, 1996.

60 Wachter, K. W., Hammel E. A., and Laslett, P. (eds), *Statistical Studies of Historical Social Structure*, Academic Press, New York, 1978.

DEMOGRAPHIC STUDIES

61 Dyer, A., 'Bastardy and prenuptial pregnancy in a Cheshire town during the eighteenth century', *Local Population Studies*, 49, 1992.

62 Glass, D. V., and Eversley, D. E. C. (eds), *Population in History: Essays in Historical Demography*, Edward Arnold, London, 1965.

63 Hollingsworth, T. H., 'The demography of the English peerage', *Population Studies*, 18 (supplement), 1964.

64 Laslett, P., *Family Life and Illicit Love in Earlier Generations: Essays in Historical Sociology*, Cambridge University Press,, Cambridge, 1972.

65 Laslett, P., Oosterveen, K., and Smith, R. M. (eds), *Bastardy and its Comparative History*, Edward Arnold, London, 1980.

66 Rotherberg, R. I., and Rabb, T. K. (eds), *Population and Economy: Population and History from the Traditional to the Modern World*, Cambridge University Press, Cambridge, 1986.

67 Schofield, R. S., 'The representativeness of family reconstitution', *Local Population Studies*, 8, 1972.

68 Schofield, R. S., 'English marriage patterns revisited', *Journal of Family History*, 10, 1985.

69 Scott, J., and Tilly, L., *Women's Work and the Family in Nineteenth-century Europe*, Studies in Society and History, 17, 1975.

70 Soulden, D., 'Movers and stayers in family reconstitution populations', *Local Population Studies*, 33, 1984.

71 Weir, D. R., 'Rather never than late: celibacy and age at marriage in English cohort fertility, 1541–1871', *Journal of Family History*, 9, 1990.

72 Wrigley, E. A., 'Family limitation in pre-industrial England', *Economic History Review*, 19, 1966.

73 Wrigley, E. A., and Schofield, R. S., *The Population History of England 1541–1871: A Reconstruction*, Edward Arnold, London, 1981, 1989.

LIFE CYCLE AND LIFE COURSE

74 Berkner, L. K., 'Rural family organisation in Europe: a problem in comparative history', *Peasant Studies Newsletter*, 1, 1972.

75 Berkner, L. K., 'The use and misuse of census data for the historical analysis of family structure', *Journal of Interdisciplinary History*, 5, 1975.

76 Bryman, A., Bythewas, W., Allatt, P., and Keil, T. (eds), *Rethinking the Life Cycle*, Macmillan, Basingstoke, 1987.

77   Chaytor, M., 'Household and kinship: Ryton in the late sixteenth and early seventeenth centuries', *History Workshop Journal*, 10, 1980.

78   Cressy, D., *Birth, Marriage and Death: Ritual, Religion, and the Life Cycle in Tudor and Stuart England*, Oxford University Press, Oxford, 1997.

79   Erickson, A. L., *Women and Property in Early Modern England*, Routledge, London, 1993.

80   Glick, P. C., and Parke, R., 'New approaches in studying the life cycle of the family', *Demography*, 2, 1965.

81   Hareven, T. K., 'The family as process: the historical study of the family cycle', *Journal of Social History*, 7, 1974.

82   Hareven, T. K. (ed.), *Transitions, the Family and the Life Course in Historical Perspective*, Academic Press, New York, 1978.

83   Levine, D., *Family Formation in an Age of Nascent Capitalism*, Academic Press, New York, 1977.

INHERITANCE

84   Bonfield, L., 'Affective families and strict settlements in early modern England', *English Historical Review*, 39, 1986.

85   Clay, C., 'Marriage, inheritance, and the rise of large estates in England, 1660–1815', *Economic History Review*, 2nd series, 21, 1968.

86   Erickson, A. L., *Women and Property in Early Modern England*, Routledge, London, 1993.

87   Faith, R., 'Peasant families and inheritance customs in the later middle ages', *Agricultural History Review*, 14, 1966.

88   Hoyle, R. W., 'The land–family bond in England', *Past and Present*, 146, 1995.

89   Larmintie, V., 'Settlement and sentiment: inheritance and personal relationships among two Midland gentry families in the seventeenth century', *Midland History*, 12, 1987.

90   Macfarlane, A., *The Origins of English Individualism: The Family, Property and Social Transition*, Cambridge University Press, Cambridge, 1979.

91   Spufford, M., 'Peasant inheritance custons and land distribution in Cambridgeshire from the sixteenth to the eighteenth centuries', in Goody, J., Thirsk, J., and Thompson, E. P. (eds), *Family and Inheritance: Rural Society in Western Europe, 1200–1800*, Cambridge University Press, Cambridge, 1976.

92   Sreenivasen, G., 'The land–family bond at Earls Colne (Essex) 1550–1650', *Past and Present*, 131, 1991.

93   Thirsk, J., 'Younger sons in the seventeenth century', *History*, 54, 1969.

94   Vann, T. K., 'Wills and the family in an English town: Banbury, 1550–1800', *Journal of Family History*, 4, 1979.

KINSHIP

95   Coster, W., *Kinship and Inheritance in Early Modern England: Three Yorkshire Parishes*, Borthwick Papers, 82, 1993.

96   Coster, W., ' "From fire and water": the responsibilities of godparents in early modern England', *Studies in Church History*, 31, 1994.

97   Coster, W., ' "To bring them up in the fear of God": guardianship in the Diocese of York, 1509–1668', *Continuity and Change*, 10, 1995.

98   Coster, W., *Baptism and Spiritual Kinship in Early Modern England*, Ashgate, London, forthcoming.

99   Cressy, D., 'Kinship and kin interaction in early Modern England', *Past and Present*, 113, 1986.

100 Hill, C., 'Sex, marriage and the family in England', *Economic History Review*, 31, 1978.

101 Mitson, A. 'The significance of kinship networks in the seventeenth century: south-west Nottinghamshire', in Phythian-Adams, C. (ed.), *Societies, Culture and Kinship 1580–1850*, Leicester University Press, Leicester, 1993.

102 Razi, Z., 'The myth of the immutable English family', *Past and Present*, 140, 1993.

103 Smith, R. M., 'Kin and neighbours in a thirteenth-century Suffolk community', *Journal of Family History*, 4, 1979.

104 Westhauser, K. E., 'Friendship and family in early modern England: the sociability of Adam Eyre and Samuel Pepys', *Journal of Social History*, 27, 1994.

105 Wolfram, S., *In-Laws and Outlaws: Kinship and Marriage in England*, Croom Helm, London, 1987.

106 Wrightson, K., 'Household and kinship in sixteenth- and seventeenth-century England', *History Workshop Journal*, 12, 1981.

YOUTH

107 Ben-Amos, I., *Adolescence and Youth in Early Modern England*, Yale University Press, New Haven, CT, 1994.

108 Brigden, S., 'Youth and the English Reformation', *Past and Present*, 95, 1982.

109 Gibbs, G. G., 'Child marriages in the Diocese of Chester, 1561–1565', *Journal of Local and Regional Studies*, 8, 1988.

110 Gillis, J. R., *Youth and History: Tradition and Change in European Age Relations 1770–Present*, Academic Press, New York, 1974.

111 Green, I., ' "For children in years and children in understanding": the emergence of the English catechism under Elizabeth and the early Stuarts', *Journal of Ecclesiastical History*, 37, 1986.

112 Griffiths, P., *Youth and Authority: Formative Experiences in England, 1560–1640*, Oxford University Press, Oxford, 1996.

113 Kussmaul, A., *Servants in Husbandry in Early Modern England*, Cambridge University Press, Cambridge, 1981.

114 Meldrum, T., *Domestic Service and Gender 1660–1750: Life and Work in the London Household*, Longman, London, 2000.

115 Mitterauer, M., *A History of Youth*, Blackwells, Oxford, 1986.

116 Pelling, M., 'Apprenticeship, health and social cohesion in early modern London', *History Workshop Journal*, 37, 1994.

117 Pollock, L., 'Younger sons in Tudor and Stuart England', *History Today*, 39, 1989.

118   Seaver, P., 'A social contract? Master against servant in the Court of Requests', *History Today*, 39, 1989.

119   Sharpe, J. A., 'Domestic homicide in early modern England', *Historical Journal*, 24, 1981.

120   Smith, S. R., 'London apprentices as seventeenth-century adolescents', *Past and Present*, 61, 1973.

121   Tudor, P., 'Religious instruction for children and adolescents in the early English Reformation', *Journal of Ecclesiastical History*, 34, 1984.

122   Wall, R., 'The age at leaving home', *Journal of Family History*, 3, 1978.

123   Wright, S. J., 'Confirmation, catechism and communion: the role of the young in the post-Reformation church', in Wright, S. J. (ed.), *Parish Church & People: Local Studies in Lay Religion*, Hutchinson, London, 1988.

124   Yarbough, A., 'Apprentices as adolescents in seventeenth-century Bristol', *Journal of Social History*, 13, 1979.

GENDER

125   Amussen, S. D., *An Ordered Society: Gender and Class in Early Modern England*, Columbia University Press, New York, 1993.

126   Fletcher, A., *Gender, Sex and Subordination in England 1500–1800*, Yale University Press, New Haven, CT, 1995.

127   Foyster, E. A., *Manhood in Early Modern England: Honour, Sex and Marriage*, Longman, London, 1999.

128   Goldberg, P. J. P. (ed.), *Women in English Medieval Society*, Sutton, London, 1997.

129   Gowing, L., 'Gender and the language of insult in early modern London', *History Workshop Journal*, 34, 1984.

130   Gowing, L., *Domestic Dangers: Women, Work and Sex in Early Modern London*, Oxford University Press, Oxford, 1996.

131   Hindle, S., 'The shaming of Margaret Knowsley: gossip, gender and the experience of authority in early modern England', *Continuity and Change*, 9, 1994.

132   Laurence, A., *Women in England 1500–1760: A Social History*, Weidenfeld and Nicolson, London, 1994.

133   Mate, M. E., *Women in Medieval English Society*, Cambridge University Press, Cambridge, 1999.

134   Mendelson, S., and Crawford, P., *Women in Early Modern England*, Oxford University Press, Oxford, 1998.

SEXUALITY

135   Bray, A., 'Homosexuality and the signs of male friendship in Elizabethan England', *History Workshop Journal*, 29, 1990.

136   Capp, B., 'The double standard revisited: plebeian women and male sexual reputation in early modern England', *Past and Present*, 162, 1999.

137   Cummins, J. S., 'Pox and paranoia in Renaissance Europe: the impact of syphilis', *History Today*, 38, 1988.

138 Fox, A., 'Ballads, libels and popular ridicule in Jacobean England', *Past and Present*, 145, 1995.

139 Hair, P. E. H., 'Bridal pregnancy in rural England in earlier centuries', *Population Studies*, 20, 1966.

140 Hair, P. E. H., 'Bridal pregnancy in earlier rural England further examined', *Population Studies*, 24, 1970.

141 Henderson, A., *Disorderly Women in Eighteenth-century London: Prostitution and Control in the Metropolis, 1730–1830*, Longman, London, 1999.

142 Herrup, C., 'The patriarch at home: the trial of the second Earl of Castlehaven for rape and sodomy', *History Workshop Journal*, 41, 1996.

143 Ingram, M., 'Ridings, rough music and the "reform of popular culture" in early modern England', *Past and Present*, 105, 1984.

144 Ingram, M., *Church Courts, Sex and Marriage in England, 1570–1640*, Cambridge University Press, Cambridge, 1987.

145 Karras, R. M., *Common Women, Prostitution and Sexuality in Medieval England*, Oxford University Press, Oxford, 1996.

146 Quaife, G. R., *Wanton Wenches and Wayward Wives*, Croom Helm, London, 1979.

147 Sharpe, J. A., *Defamation and Sexual Slander in Early Modern England: The Church Courts at York*, Borthwick Pamphlets, 58, York, 1980.

148 Thomas, K., 'The double standard', *Journal of the History of Ideas*, 20, 1959.

149 Thomas, K., 'Puritans and adultery: the Act of 1650 reconsidered', in Pennington, D., and Thomas, K. (eds), *Puritans and Revolutionaries. Essays in Seventeenth-century History Presented to Christopher Hill*, Oxford University Press, Oxford, 1978.

150 Trumbach, R., 'London's sodomites', *Journal of Social History*, 11, 1977.

151 Warnicke, R., 'Sexual heresy at the court of Henry VIII', *Historical Journal*, 30, 1987.

MARRIAGE

152 Carlson, E., 'Courtship in Tudor England', *History Today*, 42, 1993.

153 Carlson, E., *Marriage in the English Reformation*, Blackwells, Oxford, 1996.

154 Chapman, C. R., and Litton, P. M., *Marriage Laws, Rites, Records and Customs*, Lochin Publishing, Dursley, 1996.

155 Davidoff, L., and Hall, C., *Family Fortunes, Men and Women of the English Middle Class 1780–1850*, Routledge, London, 1987.

156 Durston, C., 'Unhallowed wedlocks: the regulation of marriage during the English Revolution', *Historical Journal*, 31, 1988.

157 Erickson, A. L., 'Common law versus common practice: the use of marriage settlements', *Economic History Review*, 43, 1990.

158 Fissell, M., 'Gender and generation: representing reproduction in early modern England', *Gender and History*, 7, 1995.

159 Gillis, J. R., *For Better, For Worse: British Marriages, 1600 to the Present*, Oxford University Press, Oxford, 1985.

160 Hunt, J. M., 'Wife beating, domesticity and women's independence in eighteenth-century London', *Gender and History*, 4, 1992.

161   Laramine, V., 'Marriage and the family: the example of the seventeenth-century Newdigates', *Midland History*, 9, 1984.
162   Macfarlane, A., *Marriage and Love in England: Modes of Reproduction 1300–1840*, Blackwells, Oxford, 1986.
163   O'Hara, D., ' "Ruled by my friends": aspects of marriage in the Diocese of Canterbury, *c.* 1540–1570', *Continuity and Change*, 6, 1991.
164   Outhwaite, R. B., *Clandestine Marriage in England 1500–1850*, Hambleton, London, 1995.
165   Phillips, R., *Putting Asunder: A History of Divorce in Western Society*, Cambridge, University Press, Cambridge, 1988.
166   Phillips, R., 'Divorced, beheaded, died', *History Today*, 43, 1993.
167   Schofield, R. S., and Wrigley, E. A., 'Remarriage intervals and the effect of marriage order on fertility', in Dupâquiert, J., Hélin, E., Laslett, P., Livi-Bacci, M., and Sogner, S. (eds), *Marriage and Remarriage in Populations of the Past*, Academic Press, London, 1981.
168   Shammas, C., 'The domestic environment in early modern England and America', *Journal of Social History*, 14, 1980.
169   Slater, M., 'The weightiest business: marriage in an upper-gentry family in seventeenth-century England', *Past and Present*, 72, 1976.
170   Stone, L., *The Road to Divorce: England 1530–1987*, Oxford University Press, Oxford, 1990.
171   Stone, L., *Uncertain Unions: Marriage in England 1660–1753*, Oxford University Press, Oxford, 1995.
172   Wall, A., 'Elizabethan precept and feminine practice: the Thynne family of Longleat', *History*, 75, 1990.
173   Wrigley, E. A., 'Clandestine marriage in Tetbury in the late seventeenth century', *Local Population Studies*, 10, 1973.

CHILDBIRTH

174   Berry, B. M., and Schofield, R. S., 'Age at baptism in pre-industrial England', *Population Studies*, 25, 1971.
175   Biller, P., 'Childbirth in the middle ages', *History Today*, 36, 1986.
176   Coster, W., 'Purity, profanity and Puritanism: the churching of women 1500–1700', *Women in the Church*, Studies in Church History, 27, 1990.
177   Cressy, D., 'Purification, thanksgiving and the churching of women in post-Reformation England', *Past and Present*, 141, 1993.
178   Rusden, J., 'The secret "iron tongs" of midwifery', *Historian*, 30, 1991.
179   Schofield, R. S., 'Perinatal mortality in Hawkshead, Lancashire 1581–1710', *Local Population Studies*, 4, 1970.
180   Schofield, R. S., 'Did the mothers really die? Three centuries of maternal mortality in the World we have lost', in Bonfield, L., Smith, R. M., and Wrightson, K. (eds), *The World We Have Gained: Histories of Population and Social Structure. Essays Presented to Peter Laslett on his Seventieth Birthday*, Oxford University Press, Oxford, 1986.
181   Smith-Bannister, S., *Names and Naming Patterns in England 1538–1700*, Oxford University Press, Oxford, 1997.

182 Tucker, N., 'Boon or burden? Baby love in history', *History Today*, 43, 1993.
183 Wilson, A., *The Making of Man-midwifery: Childbirth in England*, University College London Press, London, 1995.

PARENTHOOD AND CHILDHOOD

184 Ariès, P., *Centuries of Childhood*, Penguin, London, 1962.
185 Charlton, K., 'Mothers as educative agents in pre-industrial England', *History of Education*, 23, 1994.
186 Cunningham, H., *Children and Childhood in Western Society since 1500*, Longman, London, 1995.
187 Fields, V., 'The age of weaning in Britain', *Journal of Biosocial Science*, 14, 1982.
188 Fields, V. (ed.), *Women as Mothers in Pre-Industrial England. Essays in Honour of Dorothy McLaren*, Routledge, London, 1990.
189 Hanawalt, B., *Growing Up in Medieval London: The Experience of Childhood in History*, Oxford University Press, Oxford, 1993.
190 O'Day, R., *Education and Society, 1500–1800: Social Foundations of Education in Early Modern Britain*, Longman, London, 1982.
191 Orme, N., 'The culture of children in medieval England', *Past and Present*, 141, 1993.
192 Orme, N., 'Children and the church in medieval England', *Journal of Ecclesiastical History*, 45, 1994.
193 Pinchbeck, I., and Hewitt, M. (eds), *Children in English Society. Vol. I: From Tudor Times to the Eighteenth Century*, Routledge, London, 1969.
194 Plumb, J., 'The new world of children in eighteenth-century England', *Past and Present*, 67, 1975.
195 Pollock, L., *Forgotten Children: Parent–Child Relationships 1500–1900*, Cambridge University Press, Cambridge, 1983.
196 Salmon, M., 'The cultural significance of breastfeeding and infant care in early modern England and America', *Journal of Social History*, 28, 1994.
197 Sather, K., 'Sixteenth- and seventeenth-century child-rearing: a matter of discipline', *Journal of Social History*, 22, 1989.
198 Schofield, R. S., 'Dimensions of illiteracy, 1750–1850', *Explorations in Economic History*, 10, 1972.
199 Shahar, S., *Childhood in the Middle Ages*, Routledge, London, 1990.
200 Shahar, S., 'The Boy Bishop's Feast: a case-study in church attitudes towards children in the high and late middle ages', *Studies in Church History*, 31, 1994.
201 Stone, L., 'The educational revolution in England, 1560–1640', *Past and Present*, 28, 1964.
202 Wrightson, K., 'Infanticide in earlier seventeenth-century England', *Local Population Studies*, 15, 1975.

OLD AGE AND DEATH

203 Ariès, P., *Western Attitudes Towards Death*, Marion Boyers, London, 1976.
204 Ariès, P., *The Hour of Our Death*, Allen Lane, London, 1981.

205   Beaver, D., ' "Sown in dishonour, raised in glory": death, ritual and social organisation in northern Gloucestershire 1590–1690', *Social History*, 17, 1992.

206   Cross, M. C., 'The Third Earl of Huntingdon's deathbed: a Calvinist example of the *ars moriandi*', *Northern History*, 21, 1985.

207   Daniel, C., *Death and Burial in England 1066–1550*, Routledge, London, 1997.

208   Dunn, R., ' "Monuments answerable to men's worth": burial patterns, social status and gender in late medieval Bury St Edmunds', *Journal of Ecclesiastical History*, 46, 1995.

209   Gittings, C., *Death, Burial and the Individual in Early Modern England*, Routledge, London, 1984.

210   Gordon, B., and Marshal, P. (eds), *The Place of the Dead: Death and Remembrance in Late Medieval and Early Modern Europe*, Cambridge University Press, Cambridge, 2000.

211   Houlbrooke, R. A., 'The Puritan death-bed *c*. 1560–1660', in Durston, C., and Eales, J. (eds), *The Culture of English Puritanism 1560–1700*, Macmillan, Basingstoke, 1996.

212   Houlbrooke, R. A., *Death, Religion and the Family in England 1480–1750*, Oxford University Press, Oxford, 1998.

213   Litten, J., *The English Way of Death: The Common Funeral since 1450*, Robert Hales, London, 1991.

214   Marshall, P., 'Fear, purgatory and polemic in Reformation England', in Naphy, W., and Roberts, P. (eds), *Fear in Early Modern Society*, Manchester University Press, Manchester, 1997.

215   Pelling, M., 'Old age, poverty and disability in early modern Norwich', in Pelling, M., and Smith, R. M. (eds), *Life, Death and the Elderly*, Routledge, London, 1991.

216   Porter, S., 'From death to burial in seventeenth-century England', *Local History*, 23, 1993.

217   Schofield, R. S., 'Perinatal mortality in Hawkshead, Lancashire 1581–1710', *Local Population Studies*, 4, 1970.

218   Shahar, S., *Growing Old in the Middle Ages: 'Winter Clothes us in Shadowed Pain'*, Routledge, London, 1995, 1997.

219   Todd, B. J., 'The remarrying widow: a stereotype reconsidered', in Prior, M. (ed.), *Women in English Society, 1500–1800*, Methuen, London, 1985.

220   Wilson, J., 'Icons of unity', *History Today*, 43, 1993.

THE IMPACT OF IDEAS

221   Bossy, J., 'The Counter-Reformation and the people of Catholic Europe', *Past and Present*, 40, 1970.

222   Bossy, J., *Christianity in the West 1400–1700*, Oxford University Press, Oxford, 1985.

223   Crawford, P., *Women and Religion in England 1500–1720*, Routledge, London, 1993.

224 Davies, K. M., 'Continuity and change in literary advice on marriage', *Social History*, 1, 1977.

225 Foucault, M., *The History of Sexuality*, Allen Lane, London, 1978.

226 Hill, C., *Society and Puritanism in Pre-Revolutionary England*, Secker and Warburg, London, 1966.

227 Houlbrooke, R. A., *Church Courts and the People during the English Reformation, 1520–1570*, Oxford University Press, Oxford, 1979.

228 Outram, D., *The Enlightenment*, Cambridge University Press, Cambridge, 1995.

229 Ozment, S., *When Fathers Ruled: Family Life in Reformation Europe*, Harvard University Press, Cambridge, MA, 1983.

230 Rendall, J., *The Origins of Modern Feminism: Women in Britain, France and the United States, 1780–1860*, Macmillan, Basingstoke, 1985.

231 Roper, L., 'Luther, sex, marriage and motherhood', *History Today*, 33, 1983.

232 Roper, L., *Oedipus and the Devil: Witchcraft, Sexuality and Religion in Early Modern Europe*, Routledge, London, 1994.

233 Rousseau, G. S., and Porter, R. (eds), *Sexual Underworlds of the Enlightenment*, Manchester University Press, Manchester, 1987.

234 Schücking, L. L., *The Puritan Family: A Social History from the Literary Sources*, Routledge, London, 1969.

235 Todd, M., 'Humanists, Puritans and the spiritualised household', *Church History*, 44, 1980.

236 Wiesner, M. E., *Women and Gender in Early Modern Europe*, Cambridge University Press, Cambridge, 1993.

ECONOMICS

237 Anderson, M., *Family Structure in Nineteenth-century Lancashire*, Cambridge University Press, Cambridge, 1971.

238 Beer, A. L., 'Social problems in Elizabethan London', in Barry, J. (ed.), *The Tudor and Stuart Town: A Reader in Urban History 1530–1688*, Longman, London, 1990.

239 Clark, A., *The Working Life of Women in the Seventeenth Century*, Routledge, London, 1919, 1982.

240 Clark, P., 'The migrant in Kentish towns 1580–1640' in Clark, P., and Slack, P. (eds), *Crisis and Order in English Towns 1500–1700*, Routledge, London, 1972.

241 Clark, P., 'Migration in England during the late seventeenth century', *Past and Present*, 83, 1979.

242 Clark, P., and Slack, P., *English Towns in Transition, 1500–1700*, Oxford University Press, Oxford, 1976.

243 D'Cruze, P., 'Care, diligence and "useful pride": gender, industrialisation and the domestic economy, c. 1770–1840', *Women's History Review*, 3, 1984.

244 Everitt, A., 'Social mobility in early modern England', *Past and Present*, 33, 1966.

245 Harris, C. C., *The Family and Industrial Society*, Allen and Unwin, London, 1983.

246 Holderness, B. A., ' "Open" and "close" parishes in England in the eighteenth and nineteenth centuries', *Agricultural History Review*, 20, 1972.

247   Horrell, S., and Humphries, J., 'Old questions, new data, and alternative perspectives: families' living standards in the industrial revolution', *Journal of Economic History*, 294, 1992.

248   Houston, R., and Snell, K. D. M., 'Proto-industrialisation? Cottage industry, social change and Industrial Revolution', *Historical Journal*, 27, 1984.

249   Levine, D., 'Industrialisation and the proletarian family in England', *Past and Present*, 107, 1985.

250   Medick, H., 'The proto-industrial family economy: the structural function of household and family during the transition from peasant to industrial capitalism', *Social History*, 1, 1966.

251   Medick, H., *Industrialisation before Industrialisation: Rural Industry and the Genesis of Capitalism*, Cambridge University Press, Cambridge, 1976.

252   Pelling, M., 'Apprenticeship, health and social cohesion in early modern London', *History Workshop Journal*, 61, 1973.

253   Slack, P., *Poverty and Policy in Tudor and Stuart England*, Longman, London, 1988.

254   Thirsk, J., 'Industries in the countryside', in Fisher, F. J. (ed.), *Essays in the Economic and Social History of Tudor and Stuart England*, Cambridge University Press, Cambridge, 1961.

255   Thirsk, J., *The Agrarian History of England and Wales*, 4, Cambridge University Press, Cambridge, 1967.

256   Wrigley, E. A., 'A simple model of London's importance in changing English society and economy 1650–1750', *Past and Present*, 37, 1967.

INDEX

Acomb, Yorks, 17, 124–5
adultery, 66, 92
Adultery Act (1650), 93, 96
adults, 13, 26–7, 53, 58, 68, 73, 79, 83
advent, 59
affection, 12–15, 17, 66–7, 75, 86, 119
agriculture, 35, 46, 98–9, 102, 105
ale-houses, 61
almshouses, 82
altars, 83
ancestors, 13, 40, 83
Anderson, M., 7–10, 16, 28, 105
apprentices, 6, 31, 54–6, 122
apprenticeship, 51, 54–6, 78, 81, 102
architecture, 15, 18
Ariès, P., 8, 10, 13, 19, 22, 72, 74
aristocracy, 3–4, 42, 77, 97
Astel, M., 93
aunts, 40, 42–3
Austria, 23
authority, 41, 53, 55, 63, 65, 76, 81, 127
autobiography, 9, 15

Bagot family, 45
ballads, 53, 129
baptism, 24, 26–7, 40–1, 71–2, 82, 116–17, 127
Bedford, 104
begging, 82, 104–5
bells, 61, 83
Berkner, L., 23
betrothal, 58, 60–1
Bible, 16, 92
bigamy, 18, 67
Birmingham, 104
birth, 24–5, 30, 51–2, 65, 68, 70–1, 81
blessing, 61, 70, 76, 80, 115
Book of Common Prayer, 41, 120
borders, 23, 46–7
boundaries, 44, 64
Brasebridge, J., 18
breast-feeding, 68, 90
bridegrooms, 27
brides, 27, 58
Bristol, 78, 103–4

brothers, 16, 34, 43, 79
Bullinger, H., 92
burial, 24, 26, 77, 82, 84–5

cakes, 61
Calvinists, 15
Cambridge Group for the History of Population and Social Structure, 8, 22
Cambridgeshire, 75
Canterbury, 34
Capp, B., 64
catechising, 53–4
Catherine of Aragon, 41, 136
Catholicism, 16, 71, 85, 92, 126
Catholics, 26, 65, 83, 85, 92–3
celibacy, 92
census-type materials, 22–3, 25
chantries, 83
chapbooks, 53
chapels, 83
'charavari', 63
charity, 35, 82, 104
chastity, 62
Chaytor, M., 10, 44
Cheshire, 25, 63
childbirth, 68, 70–1, 129
children, 6, 9–10, 13–17, 22–5, 28, 31–4, 37, 39–40, 42, 45–6, 51–3, 55–8, 62, 65, 67–83, 85, 90, 92, 94, 97, 99–104, 112–16, 122, 125–8, 130–1, 136–7
Christ's Hospital, London, 78
church courts, 17, 41, 63, 66, 78, 124
Church of England, 60, 71, 127, 136
churching, 65, 71
churchyards, 61, 85
civil wars, 16, 53, 82, 96
clandestine marriages, 18, 60
clans, 46
Clark, A., 36, 99
Clark, P., 105
Clifford, A., 14
coffins, 84
Collinson, P., 92
common rights, 46